A Portrait of

Jackson County, Kentucky

1858–2008

is presented to the community through the generous support of

The railroad in McKee ca. 1925. (Courtesy of the Fred De Jong family)

A Portrait of
Jackson County,
Kentucky
1858–2008

The Jackson County Development Association

Picture on the cover is of the Jackson County Courthouse in the 1930s. (Courtesy of James Earl Hays)

Pictures on the back cover:
Bonnie Peters Mills in 1938. (Courtesy of Bonnie Peters Mills)
Byron Casteel and Hershel Taylor. (Courtesy of Jane Lear)
Children in McKee, circa 1910—county jail on left. (From the Engle Collection)

Front Endsheet: View of McKee about 1890. (From the Southern Appalachian Archives, Berea College Library)

Back Endsheet: The John S. Lakes place at Wind Cave in 1925. (From the Fred De Jong Collection, courtesy of the De Jong family)

The Donning Company Publishers
184 Business Park Drive, Suite 206
Virginia Beach, VA 23462

Steve Mull, *General Manager*
Barbara Buchanan, *Office Manager*
Faye Underwood, *Editor*
Stephanie Danko, *Graphic Designer*
Derek Eley, *Imaging Artist*
Debbie Dowell, *Project Research Coordinator*
Scott Rule, *Director of Marketing*
Tonya Hannink, *Marketing Coordinator*

G. Bradley Martin, *Project Director*

Library of Congress Cataloging-in-Publication Data
A portrait of Jackson County, Kentucky, 1858-2008 / the Jackson County Development Association.
    p. cm.
  Includes bibliographical references and index.
  ISBN 978–1–57864–497–1 (hard cover : alk. paper)
 1. Jackson County (Ky.)—History. I. Jackson County Development Association.
    F457.J2P67 2008
    976.9'183—dc22
                                                        2008008143

Printed in the United States of America at Walsworth Publishing Company

Contents

Preface

This book commemorates the 150th anniversary of the founding of Jackson County. Here, the reader will catch a glimpse of how we were and how we are now, encountering ordinary people as they build the structures of their lives, both physically and spiritually. The story is told largely through pictures and is therefore a representative history, not a definitive history. The reader may find gaps in the story, but may also find a few surprises. Who knew that Bond was once called Isaacs, Kentucky?

Many people contributed to this endeavor, and the Jackson County Development Association would like to thank all who participated. Special thanks to Judy Schmitt, Carolyn York, and Karen Owens, who donated numerous hours and expertise to scanning pictures and cataloging them. Our writers were Jessica Flinchum, Billy R. Farmer, Anne Gabbard, James E. Hays, Jeff Henderson, Whitney Henderson Tobias, Vivian Marcum, April Thomas, Carolyn York, Michelle Smith, and Judy Schmitt—our thanks to them.

We are indebted to skilled editors, Barbara Mabry and Wanda Renner, and to our many content readers: Jane Lear, Billy R. Farmer, Karen Combs, Regina Brewer, Roger Williams, Gary Farmer, James E. Hays, William Smith, Martha Gabbard, and Nell Westbrook. We very much appreciate the help of the staffs of the Jackson County Extension Service, the Jackson County Public Library, the Jackson County Clerk's Office, the *Jackson County Sun*, and the *Jackson County Times*. The technical and material support of Judy Schmitt and JC TEC Industries has been instrumental in the success of this project; we appreciate their help. Also providing technical support was Mike Sandlin of Sandlin's Discount, and we thank him. We also acknowledge with gratitude Citizens Bank, Jackson County Bank, Jackson Energy, and Peoples Rural Telephone Company (PRTC) for underwriting the publication of this project.

And to Carolyn York, who never tired of searching, and usually finding, just the right picture, we say a special thanks—she is a picture sleuth without equal.

There would, of course, be no book if not for the many people who loaned us their wonderful pictures. We thank and acknowledge each one:

Bessie and Leroy Adams
Lorene Adkins
Violet Allen
Ginny Ashonosheni
Gary Bailey
Rex Bailey
Roma Baker
Ora Banks
Eldon Bowling
Dewey Brewer
Regina Brewer
Tyra Brumback
Dena Burgess
Glenna Carpenter
Mary Coffey
Ruth Morgan Combs
Phillip Curd
Datha Davidson
Carroll De Forest
Fred De Jong Family
Joyce and J.R. Dunsil
George Ferrell
Jean Fee
Jessica Flinchum
Mary Lee Flinchum
Dallas Fox
Jay Fox
Ray Fox
Fletcher Gabbard

Jewell Gabbard
Keith Gabbard
Tony Gabbard
Steve Gray
Wayne Hayes
Bruce Hays
James E. Hays
Bobby Hornsby
Susan Isaacs
Huda Jones
Ramona Jones
Jake Lainhart
Bobby Lakes
Keith Lakes
Lester Lakes
Jane Taylor Lear
Opal Loeser
Elaine Madden
Joyce Marks
Lelia Martin
Glynnwood McQueen
Ronnie McWhorter
Eddie and Patsy Miller
Bonnie Peter Mills
JoAnne Moore
Mary Thomas Moore
Fern Morgan
Jack Norris
Opal Parrett
Darryll Pingleton

Ben Powell
Nolan Powell
Margaret Rader
Marie Rader
Alice Harrison Reece
Wanda Renner
George Roach
Brenda and Ronald Rose
Paul Rose
June Sasser
Paul Sears
Howard Wayne Smith Jr.
Jim Sparks
Frank Thomas
Sarah Thompson
Brenda Tillery
Emmitt Turner
Phyllis Turner
Beulah Venable
Dennis Venable
Nell Westbrook
William Whicker
Jess Wilson
Judy Wilson
Rob Williams
Roger Williams
Sue and Larry Woolum
Carolyn York

As we talked to people and gathered pictures in the making of this book, it became apparent that we could not include all pictures or treat all subjects, but we have placed in the Jackson County Public Library all donated pictures. Perhaps future historians will find this resource of value.

View from Soaptown Road, Jackson County, Kentucky. (Photograph by Jean Fee)

Introduction
The Land and its People

Jackson County lies on the very western edge of the Central Appalachian Mountains in an area known to geologists as the Escarpment. The steep hills, towering sandstone cliffs, and narrow valleys of the northern part of the county give way in the south to rolling upland meadows. It is a land described by Daniel Boone as "...a great forest on which stood myriads of trees, some gay with blooms, others rich with fruit. Nature was here a series of wonders, and a fund of delight." (*The Adventures of Daniel Boon*, 2)

This place—this Eden—was home to various native peoples for thousands of years. Archaeologists find evidence of nomadic "Paleoindians" going back to 12,000 BC, but more permanent habitats are dated to 8,000 BC, when the climate began to warm. (Sharp and Henderson, 1997) These Archaic People lived in semi-permanent base camps and seasonal hunting and fishing camps. (One of these campsites has been found in Jackson County along Carpenter's Ridge.)

By 1,000 AD, there are signs of small plots for growing food, and fragments of clay vessels appear. By 700 AD, these Late Prehistoric People were farming in the bluegrass area in the summers and moving into the hills to hunt in the winter, seeking shelter in the sandstone rock shelters along the ridges of the Escarpment. (Ibid.)

These rock shelters not only reveal the presence of the early people through their artifacts, but also through their rock carvings, or petroglyphs. Three petroglyphs, found in the northern part of the county, have been placed on the National Register of Historic Places as monuments from prehistoric times. There are many theories about the significance of these carvings. Some think they are markers, maps, or actually some rudimentary language. Perhaps they are only ancient doodles. Whatever their original purpose, they leave for us evidence of the passage of other humans—long before our presence here.

By the time of European exploration in the New World, there appear to be no permanent settlements in the land which was to become Kentucky. It was a land much fought and hunted over by the Indians, including the Shawnee, Cherokee, Choctaws, Illinois, and Creeks; but they did not linger long, returning to their homes north of the Ohio River and south of the Cumberland. (Clark, *A History of Kentucky…*, 1960, 22)

THE EUROPEANS

As early as 1606, the French ventured into the heartland of what was to become the United States of America, and by the early 1700s, had established forts on the Detroit, Miami, and Wabash Rivers. But the French did not venture far east of the Mississippi River, thus leaving a wide territory between them and the English colonists. (Clark, *Three American Fontiers; Writings of Thomas D. Clark…*, 1968, 5) It was not until the 1700s that English traders and surveyors began exploring west of the mountains.

A typical cliff face in Jackson County demonstrates the shelters lived in by Native Americans thousands of years ago. The young men looking for artifacts are from Jess Wilson's Boy Scout troop in 1962. The cliff is on Stone Coal Branch at Birch Lick. (Courtesy of Jess Wilson)

By 1750, there were well-known paths into the interior—probably the best known of these was the Warrior's Path, which connected the Shawnee of the north and the Cherokee of the south. This trail led through the Cumberland Gap north to the Ohio River, passing close to present-day Manchester, Kentucky, and proceeding northwest through Jackson County, passing close to Gray Hawk and Sand Gap, to the headwaters of Station Camp Creek, crossing the Kentucky River near present-day Irvine, Kentucky.

Daniel Boone marked a trail into Kentucky beginning in 1769, and, by 1775, Boone's Trace (more commonly known as the Wilderness Trail) was fully marked, but was probably no more than a foot path. It followed the Warrior's Path through present-day Pineville and Flat Lick, but then left the Warrior's Path to follow a buffalo trail leading slightly westward. Passing through present-day London, Kentucky, the Wilderness Trail divided at Hazel Patch, with one branch passing very near, if not crossing, a section of what was to become Jackson County.

The carvings on this rock were made by Native Americans many years ago. Located in northern Jackson County, this petroglyph is one of three in the county which are on the National Register of Historic Places. (Courtesy of Regina Brewer)

In his *A History of the Daniel Boone National Forest* (1975), Robert Collins states that this trail was for twenty-one years the only route between Cumberland Gap and the interior of

The Indian and Explorer Trails of Kentucky

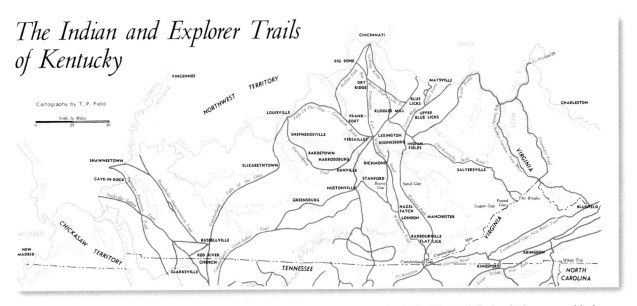

Cartography by T. P. Field

The exploration and settlement of central and eastern Kentucky owe much to both the Warrior's Path, which traversed Jackson County, north to south, and to the Wilderness Trail, or Boone's Trace. Both of these early pathways are portrayed on this map. (Reprinted with permission from *Kentucky: a Pictorial History*, J. Winston Coleman Jr., editor, 1971, University Press of Kentucky)

Kentucky. From 1775 to 1795, it is estimated that over seventy thousand people migrated into Kentucky over this route. In 1797, the Kentucky legislature authorized the building of a "state road" that would separate from the Wilderness Road at Pittsburg in Laurel County, roughly follow what is now KY 490, go down Parker's Branch and cross the Rockcastle River at what became known as Cruse Ferry. From there, the road went up White Oak Creek and joined what is now KY 1955 at the curve at the head of Trace Branch. From there it continued to Morrill and on to Milford in Madison County.

The first permanent settlement in the land that was to become Kentucky was at Harrodstown (Harrodsburg) in 1774, followed by Louisville, Washington, and Limestone (Maysville) in 1780, and Lexington in 1781. And although Indian hostilities and skirmishes with the British during the Revolutionary War made settlement hazardous, by 1783, there were over twelve thousand white settlers in the Kentucky territory, and, by 1790, there were seventy-five thousand. (Collins, 1975, 126)

Kentucky gained statehood in 1792 and was divided into nine counties. As the state became more populated, more counties were formed. By 1818, there were 59 counties, and by 1855, 103 counties. Jackson County, named for President Andrew Jackson, was formed in 1858. The last county was created in 1912 when McCreary made it 120 counties in the state.

The following chapters tell the story of the founding of Jackson County, the development and growth of communities, of churches and schools, and the industries and infrastructure which sustained them. Also included are chapters about fun times and war times.

Although this picture was taken in 1924, the homestead it portrays cannot be far different from early cabins erected by the new settlers. A one-room log cabin, probably without glass for the windows, would have provided the first shelter for early settlers. Later, additional living space could be added, as is shown here. The people in this photograph are unidentified. (From the Fred De Jong Collection, courtesy of the De Jong family)

Early Settlers

Although Jackson County was not formed until 1858, hundreds of families lived within the confines of what would be the new borders. The Munsell map of 1818 lists the place names of Double Lick, Birch Lick, and Moores Creek as being located in what is now Jackson County, indicating that there were settlements there. The Rockcastle River, Clover Bottom Creek, Horse Lick Creek, Rock Lick Creek, Pond Creek, Indian Lick Creek (Indian Creek), Laurel Fork, Granny Dismal, Wild Dog, Station Camp, and other waterways are listed, which would mean they were of some importance and had been explored. Although the Lee map of 1851 shows a road going through present-day McKee, it headed east toward Sexton's Creek instead of south to Manchester. Items of this nature are valuable because they are indicative of trading and migration patterns of European settlers as well as the ancient people before them.

And it would be along these early trails that people settled. One such trail was the current "State Road" that follows the ridge that is the Jackson-Rockcastle County line. Along this route were several inns and mills. The Moody Tavern, about a mile from Big Hill, was constructed in the early 1800s. Just south of Three Links was built the Butterfield Stage Tavern around 1817. The Cox-Simpson House, which is now the Big Hill Welcome Center, was constructed about 1840. This route was widely used as a gateway to the Bluegrass and was the road used by troops in the Civil War. The Daugherty, Moody, Cox, Martin, Ballard, McGuire, and Phillips families were early settlers in this area.

The State Road followed Horse Lick Creek for a mile or so before going up White Oak Creek. Horse Lick Creek was therefore settled going upstream from the confluence with the Rockcastle River and was settled coming downstream as well because its headwaters on Clover Bottom Creek reached to the current junction of US 421 and KY 1955. Mills were constructed at several places on Horse Lick, notably below the mouths of Raccoon, Dry Fork, and White Oak Creeks. The lower reaches of Horse Lick Creek were settled by the Durham and French families, while the Carpenter, Bowles, and Phillips families settled upstream. Clover Bottom Creek near the confluence of Horse Lick was settled in the mid-1800s by the Lakes family, who received several land grants for that area.

The upper part of Clover Bottom Creek, along what is now US 421, was settled early in Kentucky's history because of its proximity to the outer Bluegrass and the State Road. The first church in Jackson County was established at Clover Bottom sometime before 1842.

The Rose and Lainhart families were early settlers in the Rock Lick and Chestnut Flat area of Jackson County. Standing in front of their home in about 1900, are Mary Elizabeth Lainhart Rose and A. B. (Alvin) Rose. A. B. was the son of John Rose and Samaira Becknell Rose; and Mary Elizabeth was the daughter of Archibald Cassius Lainhart— one of the first elected officials of Jackson County. (Courtesy of Carolyn York)

The northern part of Jackson County, including Hisel, Rock Lick, Chestnut Flat, and Kirby Knob, is fairly close to the State Road that descended Big Hill, close to the road that went down Owsley Fork, and also close to trails over the mountain to Red Lick. This proximity to various roads led to fairly early settlement of the flat land on the ridge tops and also the fertile creek bottoms of Rock Lick and Station Camp Creeks. Much of this land was owned by landholders from the Bluegrass area in the early 1800s; but by the time that Jackson had become a county, or shortly thereafter, the Rose, Isaacs, Williams, Kerby, Hisel, Powell, Harrison, Collins, and Lainhart families had settled there.

Several Lakes families also lived on Lakes Creek, near Wind Cave, in what was originally Estill County. According to the late Julia Lakes Isaacs, her great grandfather, Carter Lakes, was settled in the area before the "year the stars fell." This puts the family here before 1833, which was the year that a large meteor shower was visible from the eastern United States.

Indian Creek, stretching from McKee to its confluence with Laurel Fork (the two of which form Middle Fork of the Rockcastle River), was an important area of early settlement. The area of Middle Fork was home to Jackson County's first County Judge, Isaac Faubus, and also home to the Tussey, Angel, Gabbard, and Stephens families.

The area that is now Tyner and Egypt was part of Clay County, so many of the residents there today have more relatives in Clay than in Jackson. The Wilson, Baker, Halcomb, Davidson, Jones, and Pennington families were among the early settlers in this area.

The region between Tyner and Manchester was settled very early in the 1800s because of its proximity to the Warrior's Path and the Manchester Salt Works. The Jones family of Tyner still retains much of the land settled by Dutton and Rebecca Stewart Jones before 1850. The town of Gray Hawk is also near the Warrior's Path and at the crossroads of a trail that connected Laurel Fork and Indian Creek in central Jackson County to the rolling farmland of the eastern part, near Clay and Owsley Counties, which were settled more densely and earlier than Jackson. The Hays family moved to Gray Hawk and settled a large tract of land on the waters of McCammon Creek before 1850, and many descendents still reside there. Other families which were among the first settlers were Casteel, Fowler, McQueen, and Parris. (Collins, 1874, v.2, 353)

Ambrose and Kizzie Brockman raised a family of nine children in the Horse Lick/Sand Gap area of Jackson County. Ambrose was born on Horse Lick about 1852. (Courtesy of Sarah Thompson)

The first Jackson County census in 1860 listed 513 households with the following surnames: Abner, Abrams, Alexander, Allen, Ambrose, Amix, Anderson, Andrew, Angel, Arnolds, Arthur, Atkins, Azbell, Bails, Baker, Bales, Ballard, Barrett, Barnett, Becknell, Benge, Biggs, Blanton, Bowles, Bowman, Brewner, Brockman, Browning, Brummit, Bullack, Cain, Callahan, Candee, Cornelious, Carpenter, Carroll, Carter, Cassady, Casteel, Cates, Clark, Clemins, Coyle, Cole, Coleman, Collins, Comes, Cook, Cope, Cotton, Cox, Crawford, Culton, Cunnigan, Davis, Dean, Deaton, Dees, Denim, Dennel, Drew, Duncan, Durham, Edwards, Elkins, Engle, Ervin, Estill, Evans, Farmer, Farthing, Faubus, Flanery, Flinn, Fowler, Franc, Freeman, French, Frost, Gabbard, Gabbet, Gay, Gilbert, Glenn, Gooch, Golden, Goodman, Green, Griffin, Gumm, Halcomb, Hale, Hall, Hamilton, Hammons, Harrison, Hays, Hazelwood, Hellard, Hill, Hillard, Hilton, Himes, Hisel, Horn, Hornsby, Howard, Hubbard, Hudson, Hughes, Hunt, Hunter, Hurley, Hurst, Hutson, Inman, Isaacs, Jackson, Jiles, Johnson, Jones, Kallin, Kelly, Kenny, Kerby, Kursey, Kidd, King, Kiplinger, Lakes, Lanehart, Laws, Lawsin, Lear, Lewis, Little, Logsdon, Lunsford, Lunts, McCollum, McQueen, McWhorter, Madden, Magee,

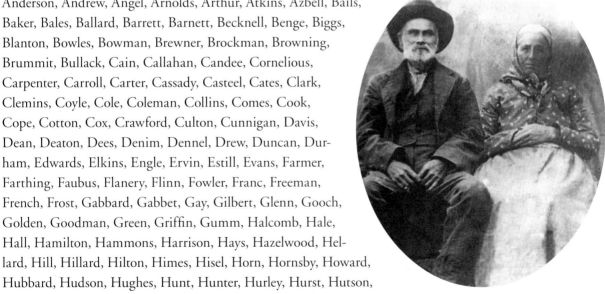

Isaac (1813–1915) and Mary Clouse Madden came from Mulberry Gap, Tennessee, and settled at Herd, Kentucky, in 1852. He worked for John Farmer as a sharecropper. (Courtesy of Wayne Hayes)

Robert and Mary Jane Phillips McQueen, who raised a family of seven children in the Salt Rock area of the county, are pictured here about 1895. Jane, born in 1839, was the daughter of Thomas and Edy Gumm Phillips. According to family tradition, Robert, the son of John and Rachel Sparks McQueen, was born in McKee in 1835 on land now occupied by the Jackson County Courthouse. (Courtesy of Dewey Brewer)

Alexander Frank Hays, a Civil War veteran and son of Robert and Nancy Hays, is pictured here with his wife, Wilmouth Hudson Hays, and an unidentified child. The Hays Family settled in the Gray Hawk area about 1850. Robert Hays was elected County Judge of Jackson County in 1867. (Courtesy of Wayne Hays)

Mahaffey, Mahcon, Marcum, Martin, Meguire, Melborn, Metcalfe, Miller, Millian, Millman, Miracle, Moberly, Montgomery, Moore, Morris, Mullins, Murphy, Nealy, Newman, Nichoals, Owens, Parker, Parks, Parris, Parrett, Parsons, Pennington, Phillips, Pigg, Portwood, Powell, Pucketts, Purvis, Rader, Radford, Ramsey, Rector, Reece, Reed, Riddle, Robards, Roberts, Robins, Robinson, Rogers, Rose, Runnels, Sandlin, Sea, Seaborn, Seals, Simpson, Skinner, Slagel, Sloan, Smith, Sparks, Spivey, Spurlin, Stapleton, Stephens, Stewart, Summers, Sutles, Taylor, Thompson, Tillery, Tincher, Truet, Turner, Tussey, Underwood, Vance, VanWinkle, Ward, Webb, West, Wyatt, Wicker, Wilder, Williams, Willis, Wilson, Witt, Wood, and Young.

The spellings of the family names listed above and elsewhere in this history vary depending on the person writing the document (in this case the census taker) and on the time it was written, as name spellings changed over time. Some family names in the 1860 census are represented many times over, indicating a rather early migration to this area. There were eighteen households of the Isaacs family, fourteen Powell families, twelve families of Faubus, and nine households of the Baker, Williams, and Lakes families. On the other hand, there was only one household each of the Parrett, Hays, and Hisel families, perhaps indicating that they were newly arrived in the county. Today, however, they represent many residents of Jackson County.

The 1860 census also revealed the occupations of a few residents, or more likely the occupations that were considered of value or status to society at the time. There were three heads of household that were listed as carpenters: James Angel, Henry Wilder, and Allen Summers. Six men were listed as Baptist ministers, including Henry Morris, Andrew Isaacs, Hardin Sloan, Edward Baker, Preston Pennington, and Thomas Robinson. Thomas Bowman and his son were Methodist ministers, and John Ward was listed as a minister. Four residents were blacksmiths, including Thomas Lakes, Joshua Coleman, and Isaac Faubus, and eighty-eight-year-old Thomas Marcum. Physician George Edwards, surveyor Phillip Marcum, teacher Henry Stewart, attorney Robert Hays, merchant James Vance, and farmer William Metcalfe rounded out the list of those whose occupations were noted. Two persons were listed as domestics. County officials listed were Sheriff John Stephens, Constable John Morris, and County Judge Isaac Faubus. It may be assumed that those whose occupations were not listed were engaged in subsistence farming, including hunting and small-scale logging.

James Hays, a Civil War veteran and brother to Alexander Frank Hays, is shown here with his wife, Frances Jones Hays. They lived in a large house located across the road from where the Jackson County Bank now sits, and rented out rooms to boarders. James also ran a store in McKee. (Courtesy of Nell Hays Westbrook)

The typical household in 1860 usually consisted of two parents, six to ten children, and, frequently, an aged parent or other relative. Priorities were to keep an adequate food supply for the family. Most families raised a large garden in the rich creek bottom soil and had their own spring. Chickens dotted the barnyard and pigs foraged in the woods until rounded up for sale or slaughter. There was at least one person in every community who made molasses and a mill that ground corn on every large creek. Centuries-old methods of preserving food were used, including drying and sulfuring fruits or burying cabbage, turnips, and potatoes under the floor of the house or in a pit in the barn. Every community had smokehouses where hams were smoked for use all winter. Cabbage and cucumbers were soaked in brine for kraut and pickles. Canning was not as common as it is now because it was not as reliable as other methods. Treasured items that early settlers brought with them were starts of apple and peach trees that had been cultivated in their home state. Some of these varieties still exist on old Jackson County farmsteads. Although life could be hard and certainly required hard work, nineteenth century Jackson Countians were sustained by a strong sense of community.

The following chapters will describe the founding of the county, the growth of communities, the development of social and economic institutions, and the changes that have occurred in 150 years.

Matilda Gabbard Lakes lived in the Wind Cave area with her husband, Murrill Lakes, who was the son of Carter and Eady Lakes, very early settlers on Lakes Creek. (Courtesy of Dewey Brewer)

Gathered in front of the second Jackson County Courthouse about 1890 are citizens who have come to town for "Court Day." (Courtesy of June Sasser)

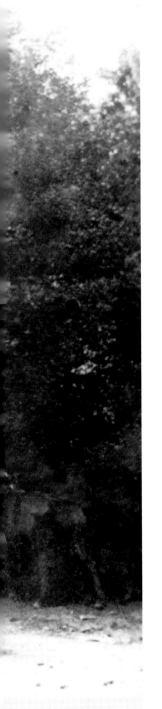

The Founding

Jackson County and the county seat, McKee, were established by decree of the state legislature on April 15, 1858. The county, formed from parts of the existing counties of Rockcastle, Owsley, Madison, Clay, Estill, and Laurel, was named for Andrew Jackson, the seventh president of the United States and the first to be elected from west of the Appalachians. According to Collins' *History of Kentucky* (1874), the county seat was named after Judge George R. McKee.

In March of 1858, six representatives of the mother counties (T. T. Garrard, James D. Ballard, Ruebin Monday, James E. Gibson, R. T. Benton, and Levi Jackson) met and recorded the following:

> We, the undersigned commissioners appointed by an act of the general assembly of the commonwealth of Kentucky to locate the town of McKee in the county of Jackson did on the 4th Monday in March 1858 meet at the house of John Morris and after being duly sworn to faithfully discharge the duties assigned us proceeded to locate the same opposite the mouth of Bills Branch on Indian Creek on the Lands of Solomon Stephens this the 23rd day of March 1858. (*Court Order Book 1*, 10)

In the same meeting, M. C. Hughes was appointed to survey the boundary line of the county and to prepare plans for the county seat.

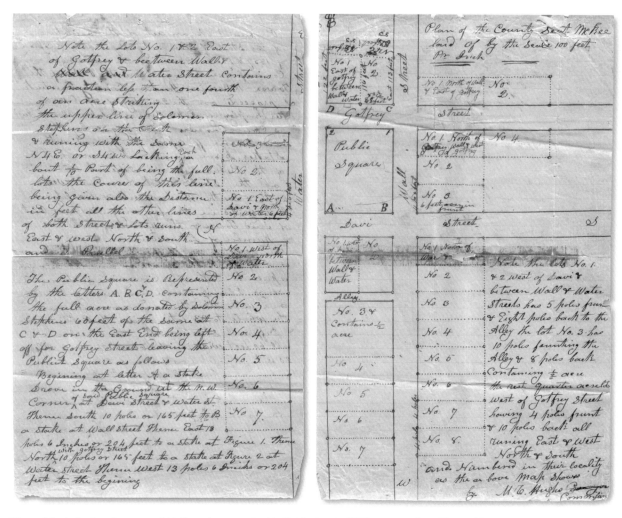

The original plat for the town of McKee, drawn up by M. C. Hughes in 1858, is reproduced here. (Courtesy of Regina Brewer)

Also appointed were commissioners to lay off the boundaries of "six election districts and justice districts." These commissioners (John Morris, Robert Hays, Morgan Faubus, George W. Rogers, Carter Lakes, and John Farmer) met several times, first at Soloman Stephens' house and then at John Morris' house, and appear to have had some difficulty in agreeing on boundaries:

> …after several unsuccessful efforts to lay of and designate the boundry lines of the middle and Town districts of Said county of Jackson We again adjourned until Thursday morning at nine oclock 25 March 1858 The commissioners met in pursuance of adjournment at the house of John Morris and again proceded to business. John Morris and Robert Hays asked leave to with draw from the board which was granted on condition that they would each of them sign the procedings and certificates of the boundry of the several districts, as laid off by the others and Remaining members of the board… Proceded to lay off and district the county of Jackson into six Election precincts and Justice districts… [note: all spellings are as written in the original] (Ibid., 11)

With boundaries established, the justices proceeded to hold the first county election on May 1, 1858. Elected were: Isaac J. Faubus, county judge; Thomas J. Engle, county court clerk, and circuit court clerk; Alfred Willson (in other places in the order book this is spelled Alford Wilson), sheriff; Hiram Bundnen, coroner; Philip Marcum, surveyor; and John Anglin, jailor. Constables were also elected, including A. C. Lainheart, John Robertson, and Humphrey W. Fowler. Justices elected were: C. D. Gooch, John Reece, E. W. Clark, James Lainhart, Lewis Davis, and John Lakes.

It appears that these first justices met in various homes until a courthouse could be built. The records of the May Term state:

Isaac J. Faubus was the first County Judge of Jackson County, serving from 1858–1862. He was born in 1814 in Tennessee and died in Jackson County in 1890. (Photograph reprinted from *The Rural Kentuckian,* March 1977, courtesy of Jackson Energy)

Elected in 1858 as the first Jackson County Court Clerk as well as the first Circuit Court Clerk was Thomas Jefferson Engle. He is pictured here in his Civil War uniform, having joined the Union Army in 1862 with the rank of Captain in the 47th Kentucky Mounted Infantry. He died in camp in 1863. (Courtesy of James E. Hays)

TAVERNS
■ ■ ■

In the pages of the court records of 1858 can also be found actions taken to license taverns and the selling of alcoholic beverages:

> Ordered that Anderson Willson is hereby authorized to keep a tavern at his house in Jackson County on the road leading from Booneville to London, it appearing to the satisfaction of the court that there is a tavern needing and he having entered into bond which was approved of by the court with Alford Wilson and John Marcum, and took the oath prescribed by law this 18th day of May 1858. Thos. J. Engle Clerk of Jackson County. (*Court Order Book 1*, 12)

A similar license was granted to John Reece on the road "leading from McKee to the State Road on the bigg hill [sic], he having paid the clerk of this court ten dollars.. on this 21st June 1858." (Ibid., 19) Apparently, running a tavern meant more than offering bed and breakfast, as rates for serving alcohol were also set by the court:

> Ordered that Rates of Tavern Keepers in Jackson County be as follows man and horse Supper breakfast and lodging 1.00 Single diet twenty five cents Bed per night 10 cents board per week 2.50 cents per year one hundred dollars, per day 75 cents, Single horse feed 25 cents horse to hay 10 cents, horse per day 40 cents per weak 2.50 cents Spirits per gallon (Whisky) [sic] Brandies Peach and apple 1.50 cents. Wine Rum and Gin 1.50 cents Whiskey per quart 35 cents pint 20 cents half pint 10 per drink 5 cents Brandies Wine per quart 40 cents pint 25 cents half pint 10 cents per drink 5 cents. [Note: all spellings and monetary notations are as in the original] (Ibid., 12)

Jackson County's second courthouse was a large framed building erected in 1872. It was replaced by a brick courthouse in 1924. (From the Fred De Jong Collection, courtesy of the De Jong family)

This panorama of McKee in 1924 shows the first three courthouses of Jackson County. The second courthouse, shown just to the right of the new (third) courthouse, is being dismantled. The first courthouse is the white-roofed building directly across Main Street from the new courthouse. (Courtesy of Jess Wilson and Carl Cunnagin)

It is ordered by the court that Justices now present take their seats to take in consideration the property where they will hold their next court, Justice present… agreed that the next Court at David Stephens house at the mouth of Hootens Branch. (Ibid., 14)

Also among these first orders recorded was the appointment of a committee consisting of Thomas Engle, Alfred Wilson, and John Anglin to draft a plan for a temporary courthouse. This first courthouse was built of logs and stood directly across US 421 from the present courthouse. It was built on a lot purchased from Solomon Stephens for forty dollars, to be paid in six months. (Hudson, 1996) This structure, although established as a temporary courthouse, served the county until 1872. It later became a residence and was known as the W. M. Clark house. It was demolished in 1947 or 1948.

The second courthouse, a large frame building, was built in 1872 on the public square (where the present courthouse now stands)—an acre of land donated to the county by Soloman Stephens and his wife, Margaret, in October of 1859. The square was laid off in the survey by Hughes. This second courthouse stood until 1924, when it was replaced by a brick building with stately columns. This third courthouse was severely damaged by fire in December of 1949. By the following year, it was remodeled and stands today, although it received a new brick façade in 2007.

Archibald Cassius Lainhart, who was elected Constable in the first county elections in 1858, also served in the Civil War. (Courtesy of Jake Lainhart)

The courthouse built in 1924 was heavily damaged by fire in December of 1949. This picture shows the rebuilt courthouse (1950) in 2007.

This view of McKee, about 1925, is looking toward town from the hill above the McKee Academy, whose upper story is just visible in the right hand corner. (From the Jackson County Public Library Collection)

Communities
What's in a Name?

A newcomer to Jackson County soon learns the importance of place names. And some are wonderfully descriptive: Salt Rock, Green Hill, Birch Lick, Chinquapin Rough, Rock Lick, Clover Bottom, Chestnut Flat. Others take on the names of people or families, such as Foxtown, Mildred, Moores Creek, Welchburg, or Atkinstown. And then there are Egypt and Mummie. Egypt is said to have gotten its name because early settlers, fleeing the Civil War in Tennessee, felt exiled—just like the children of Israel. As for Mummie, local legend says that a mummified body was found in a house nearby and so the name. Letterbox got its name because mail was left in a box in a hollow tree where people would come and get their mail—or so the story goes.

In early days, these place names may have designated a small collection of homesteads in a particular place—a place which could be defined by geographic characteristics or family groups living there. Cave Springs was just such a place. It grew up along Cave Springs Road, which lies just off U.S. Highway 421, between Morrill and Clover Bottom. It derived its name from the small spring there. Wanda Abrams Renner, a descendant of the early settlers, describes the spring: "There was a cave that went back into the hillside. It wasn't large enough for anyone to walk in but possibly large enough for someone to crawl back in. There was water coming from that cave. A barrel or tub was placed in the spring to catch the water. The area at the spring was large enough that a person could walk around the tub and dip water from it with their bucket."

The "Sinks and Rises" on the South Fork of Station Camp Creek are just north of the Clover Bottom Quarry—not far from the early community of Cave Springs. Shown here, just where the creek emerges from its underground passage, are two ladies enjoying this natural wonder. (From the Southern Appalachian Archives of the Berea College Library)

This spring is thought to be a source of the South Fork of the Station Camp Creek and of the well-known "sinks and rises," which are on the other side of U.S. Highway 421. The area near the "sinks and rises" belonged to Hiram Dean. According to Dewey Abrams, Dean had a gristmill down near the sinks and rises: "that's where people went to get their corn ground. Also at the 'sinks and risings' was where people went to vote."

The community of Cave Springs never had a post office and is not on any map except as Cave Springs Road. If you travel down Cave Springs Road today you will see the one hundred-year-old Cave Springs Church and cemetery and a few farms. But once, this place was a thriving, close-knit community, comprised of general stores, a church and cemetery, a school, and several families who made their living by farming. In the early 1900s, the community also had a dentist, James Sidney Van Winkle. There was a gristmill owned by Milburn Rice and two sawmills—one owned by Granville Hayes and another by Winfred Van Winkle and Ellis Shearer.

Hiram Dean, pictured with wife, Lucy, and children (Ray in back, America, Zella and baby John in front), was a prominent figure in the early 1900s. He not only ran a gristmill and sawmill on South Fork (just downstream of the Cave Springs community), but also served as Magistrate, County Attorney, and in 1920, as State Representative, 80th District. (Courtesy of Phyllis Dean Turner)

After World War II several of the general stores and sawmills closed, as the younger people left for better opportunities in the manufacturing towns north of the Ohio River. The story of Cave Springs is the story of many communities throughout the county.

It is the story of the building up of close-knit communities from pioneer beginnings, and it is the story of change as other opportunities opened up.

POST OFFICES

A community's post office played a vital role in the lives of its citizens. It served to validate their place in the county, gave them a way to communicate with each other as well with the rest of the world, and was one of the main places to gather and socialize. In the early days, the post office was often housed in the general store, with the store owner also becoming the postmaster or postmistress.

In order to establish a post office, members of a new community would generally submit a request to the Post Office Department stating the need, the number of patrons who would be served, and proposed names for the new post office. Since the citizens had such a hands-on involvement in the establishment and naming of their post office, they took a very personal ownership in it. Before 1891, the government had no written policies about naming post offices. Most often the name submitted would be the same as the community name. Sometimes, though, a new office would be named for a local person or family (sometimes for the first postmaster) or for a special landmark or geographical feature in the community.

James Sidney Van Winkle, son of Cashus Marcellus and Cordelia Azbill Van Winkle, was a dentist, operating out of his home at Cave Springs. He and his wife, Dovie Gentry Van Winkle, are shown here about 1899 with their children: Lavelle, Winfred, and Clara. (Courtesy of Wanda Renner)

Post Offices were often located in a general store. Hisel Grocery and Post Office is shown here, about 1977, with Gus Hisel, Forester Hisel, Elwood Hisel, and Wentworth Lainhart sitting on the porch. Zola Hisel served as Postmistress here from 1948 until 1980. (Courtesy of Ben Powell)

JACKSON COUNTY POPULATION

■ ■ ■

In 1860, two years after the founding of the county, there were a little over 3,000 people living here—about nine people per square mile. The population increased steadily to 4,547 in 1870, and to over 10,000 in 1900 (thirty people per square mile). The peak of population was reached in 1940—16,339 people. During and right after World War II, Jackson County lost twenty percent of its population, and another eighteen percent from 1950–60. This out-migration was repeated across eastern Kentucky as word spread of work in the factories of the North. This decline was reversed in the 1970s, and, since then, there has been a steady increase in the county's population. In 2000, population stood at 13,495. (U. S. Censuses)

The Gray Hawk Post Office, established in October 1853, was the first post office in Jackson County and is said to have been named for two men who owned a large tract of land in the area. Next came Green Hall (1855), Middle Fork (1856), Mauldin (1857, re-established as Maulden in 1884), and McKee (1858). The Nathanton Post Office, established in 1884, is thought to be named for its first post-master, Nathan Clark, while the Orpha Post Office, established in 1905 in the New Zion area, was said to be named after the wife of the first postmaster, Josephus Ward. Many post offices had their name changed sometime during their service period. Chinquapin Rough, established in 1878 and named for the Chinquapin tree that was once prevalent in Jackson County, became the Annville Post Office in 1886; and Collinsworth, established in 1886, became Sand Gap Post Office in 1902.

Located at the corner of Gotfrey and Main Streets in the early 1900s, this building served as an early post office in McKee and also as a store. Grace and Ellis Holcomb later ran a drugstore in this building. It is unknown what the large barrels contain. (From the Fred De Jong Collection, courtesy of the De Jong family)

Above: The McKee Post Office, shown here on the left about 1942, faced out onto what is now Highway 290 and sat approximately where the bank parking lot is now. The Jackson County Bank is just to the right of the post office. (Courtesy of Frank Thomas)

Left: Sitting inside the McKee Post Office in the 1930s is Postmaster Norman Thomas. (Courtesy of Frank Thomas)

Top: Sarah McQueen stands in front of the Bond Post Office around 1940. The community of Bond was originally named Isaacs, and its first post office was established in May 1899. It was renamed Bond in 1914 to honor N.U. Bond, chief owner of Bond-Foley Lumber Company. (Courtesy of Glenna Carpenter)

Above: A new McKee Post Office was built in 1999. Frank Thomas serves as Postmaster. (Photograph by Jean Fee)

During the next several decades, more than sixty new post offices were established. The years 1902 and 1905 saw the most growth. Six new offices were established in 1902: Lantana, Wind Cave, Mildred, Laura, Hurley (named for the first postmaster, William Hurley), and Lite. Five new offices were established in 1905: Datha, Double Lick, Lynch, Orpha, and Deese. According to Robert Rennick's *Jackson County, Kentucky Post Offices* (1975), there have been over seventy post offices named in Jackson County.

By 1942, only around thirty post offices were still in existence. Offices were discontinued by the government when there no longer appeared to be a public need or when a suitable postmaster could not be found. A few of the shortest-lived post offices were Ledford, whose order was rescinded after two and one-half months in 1895; Sand Bluff (1873) and Powell (1901), discontinued after eight months; and Birch Lick, discontinued after approximately eight and one-half months in 1871. It was not until 1900 that a new post office, now named Waneta, was opened in the Birch Lick area.

In recent times, the expansion of rural carrier routes, made possible by better roads, and advances in technology, which enable a greater volume of mail to be processed within each office, have allowed for a reduction in the number of post offices. In 2007, there were only five post offices in the county: McKee, Annville, Sand Gap, Gray Hawk, and Tyner. The remainder of this chapter will look at these communities.

McKee

Although the streets of McKee were laid out in the 1858 survey by Hughes, the City of McKee was not incorporated until 1881. Appointed as Trustees were James Hays, Daniel Morris, Jack Clark, Scott McGuire, and Henry Morris. A survey of the incorporated boundary lines was made by Henry Morris in 1881.

In 1938, local citizens petitioned to incorporate the town, unaware that it had already been incorporated. With the exception of the above notation in the court records, there apparently are no records of town meetings until 1938. On April 18, 1938, new trustees were appointed: J. R. Hays, J. E. Holcomb, M. V. Neeley, J. B. Wilson, and Dewey Baker, and the first town meeting of record was held. (From notes by June Sasser)

Over the years the town has grown and changed. The early 1900s saw rapid growth in McKee—the Reformed Church built a school, dormitory, and church, and the Bond-Foley Lumber Company ran a train to McKee. The town prospered, providing a valuable center of commerce for the county, with a bank, various general stores, as well as a boarding house.

In 1929, J. E. Holcomb and his wife, Grace, opened their drugstore on the corner of Gotfrey (now First Street) and Main Streets, having purchased the building, which used to house the post office, from Lloyd Sparks and his sister, Dora Little. In an interview with *The Jackson County Sun* in 1989, Mrs. Holcomb, now deceased, recalled that McKee was a different place: "In its heyday, you couldn't stir them with a stick. It was that busy. But nowadays it's a lot quieter; I remember a man shot at a man … by the

An early landmark in McKee, in the latter part of the 1800s, was the home of James and Fannie Hays. Mrs. Hays ran a boarding house here, and it is thought that a freed slave lived for many years in the upper right corner room. Known as "The Hotel," the house was located across the street from the current site of the Jackson County Bank. (Courtesy of James Earl Hays)

Water Street was sometimes known as Jockey Street because men would gather to trade and sell horses and mules. Gathered in front of the Tyra Lainhart house (at the corner of Water Street and State Highway 89 North) is such a group in 1925. (From the Fred De Jong Collection, courtesy of the De Jong family)

Jim Tompkins, founder of *The Jackson County Sun*, began his printing and newspaper business in 1926 in the little building pictured here at the intersection of Water Street and what is now Third Street. (Courtesy of Jack Norris)

THE MAN THAT MAKES T...
"SUN-SHINE"
IN MCKEE.

Jimmie The Printer

Is ready at all times to help you out on that Job of printing.

Mr. Tompkins advertised his printing business with this business card provided by his grandson, Jim Sparks.

Pictured here, about 1939, is Elizabeth Byrd Bailey coming out of Holcomb's Drugstore in McKee with one of her grandsons. Holcomb's Drugstore occupied this building at the corner of First (Gotfrey) and Main Streets from 1929–1962. The building was demolished in 2007 to make way for a new Justice Center. (Courtesy of Gary Bailey)

courthouse one time. He shot all around him (and) skimmed his (own) head with a bullet. The doctor from up at the CCC camp came by and wrapped his head up."

Grace remembered the Bond-Foley train that ran from McKee to East Bernstadt: "There used to be a railroad, just an old whistle train, it made whistle stops. I'd get on it at Summit, that was a whistle stop, and come to McKee, when I was teaching school."

Holcomb's Drugstore closed in 1962 when Mr. Holcomb died, but the building has served since in various capacities. In 2007, it was razed, along with the Holcomb house next door to make way for the Jackson County Justice Center, scheduled for completion in 2009.

Pictured here is the McKee Civilian Conservation Corps (CCC) camp, built about 1933 on land now occupied by the Bond Memorial Park and BAE Systems. The area is still known as the CCC Bottoms. (Courtesy of Regina Brewer)

The Depression of the 1930s brought a halt to the growth of the 1920s. McKee lost its railroad when the Bond-Foley Lumber Company closed in 1930, putting hundreds out of work. However, the federal assistance programs, beginning in 1933, brought an influx of funds which enabled the building of significant infrastructure in McKee and throughout the county. The Civilian Conservation Corps (CCC), which established a camp in McKee (where the Bond Memorial Park is now), built numerous roads and bridges in the county, several fire towers for the just-forming national forest, and installed a telephone line from McKee to London for the forest service. And in McKee, the CCC men built the forest service building, which still stands at the foot of Pigeon Roost Hill.

The Works Progress Administration (WPA) and its forerunner, the Civil Works Administration (CWA), also made significant contributions to the infrastructure in McKee and the county. WPA projects in McKee included the construction of four sidewalks, the grading, draining, and surfacing of all streets in McKee, two hundred linear feet of stone wall, and the construction of a new McKee High School, which opened in 1938. (Kennedy and Johnson)

Outside of McKee, CWA projects included seventeen miles of road improvement and the construction of two, two-span wooden bridges. County-wide WPA projects included the grading and draining of several roads in the county, the construction of a gymnasium at the Tyner School, and a new elementary school at Gray Hawk. An administration building for the WPA was built just beside Indian Creek on the south side of Wall Street (U.S. 421), where Smith Motors now resides.

The housing of several hundred young men in McKee, at the CCC camp, must have had an economic and social impact on the community. Perhaps the movie theater built during the tenure of the CCC camp was in response to this increase in the population of McKee. Albert Taylor, John Dunsil, and Bud Hughes were instrumental in bringing the movie theater to McKee in the 1930s. This was a popular venue for many years.

FEDERAL RELIEF PROGRAMS IN THE 1930s

■ ■ ■

To combat the vast unemployment of the 1930s, President Franklin D. Roosevelt established several work relief programs. Among them was the Civilian Conservation Corps (CCC), which was established in 1933 to give work opportunities to young, unemployed men, aged eighteen to twenty-five (later extended to age twenty-seven). From the time of Roosevelt's inauguration on March 4, 1933, to the induction of the first enrollee on April 7, only thirty-seven days had elapsed. (http://www.cccalumni.org/history1.html) Enrollees worked forty hours a week and earned about a dollar a day. They worked mostly on conservation projects such as the prevention of soil erosion, but also installed telephone and power lines, built trails within parks, and planted trees for the forest service. The Civilian Conservation Corps was disbanded in 1942 as World War II drew young men into the war effort.

Also of importance were the Civil Works Administration (CWA), 1933–34, and the Works Progress Administration (WPA), 1935–43. The CWA program hired both men and women and focused on the repair or construction of public buildings, roadways, and parks. However, the program was halted in 1934 because of its huge costs. The WPA program, a remodeled version of the CWA, also put people to work building infrastructure. During its tenure, the WPA constructed 116,000 buildings, 78,000 bridges, 651,000 miles of road, and the improvement of 800 airports throughout the United States. (The Columbia Encyclopedia, 6th edition 2001–05)

Travis Sparks remembers working in Lloyd Sparks' store in this time period. He began working for Sparks after school in his freshman year of high school and worked all during high school and for a year after graduation in 1940, when he went to Ohio to work. Travis recalls that the CCC "boys" would often come into the store:

> The boys would come into town mostly on the weekends and evenings. We sold a lot of cardboard suitcases and foot lockers to those boys. And they used to hang out at Doc Holcomb's drugstore. But the camp was run by the army, so there were lots of rules and regulations. They got $30 a month in pay, but had to send $25 of that back home, getting to keep only $5 a month (editor's note: about $70 in 2007 dollars). You know, they sent the local boys to other states, so most of these boys were from away from here.

New retail businesses also opened in the 1930s. Albert Taylor opened a furniture store in partnership with his brother, Jimmy. According to Jane Taylor Lear, her father, Albert, soon bought out Jimmy and added a dish and hardware store beside the furniture store. The library now occupies this site. John Dunsil bought out the Chevrolet dealership owned by Floyd Farmer in 1936, and, in 1949,

John Dunsil, pictured here in 1952, operated the Chevrolet dealership in McKee from 1936 until 1979. Mr. Dunsil also served in the state legislature from 1955–57. (Courtesy of Jane Taylor Lear)

built a new garage and dealership where Smith Motors is today. Competing with Dunsil's dealership was Casteel's Ford dealership, which was located where the post office is today.

The relative prosperity of the years after World War II saw growth in McKee, with the establishment of various new retail stores. This prosperity continued into the 1960s with the added improvements of a municipal water system and sewage treatment plant.

But as roads improved and people became more mobile in the 1970s and 80s, McKee lost its car dealerships, its movie theater, and several retail businesses. The competition from the larger, nearby communities of London and Richmond hurt. But these years also saw improvements. In 1973, the White House Clinic, a nonprofit community health center, was established, and, in 1983, Jack Fifield opened his dental clinic. A small park was created in 1986, just south of town on Highway 290. In 1998, this park was dedicated to the memory of Jack Gabbard, Mayor of McKee from 1984 to 1996.

From the early 1990s through 2007, McKee experienced a booming growth period, as new structures replaced many aging buildings, and old buildings were refurbished. Now housed in new buildings are Peoples Rural Telephone Cooperative (PRTC), Farm Bureau Insurance, the White House Clinic, the Extension Office, the library, the post office, the Dollar General Store, and the Family Dollar Store. By 2007, the town stretched from the foot of Pigeon Roost Hill in the east to State Highway 89 South in the west—a distance of almost two miles.

Old buildings have reinvented themselves. Among those sporting new facelifts are the Hughes block on the Courthouse Square, Campbell's Drugs, and Jackson County Bank. And new businesses and buildings have sprung up: Citizen's Bank, The Area Technology Center on Education Mountain, Sav-a-Lot Grocery, Rite-Aid, Brewer's Tax Service, Subway, and Sandlin's Discount— just to mention a few.

Albert Taylor operated a furniture store and a dish and hardware store in McKee for many years. Pictured here on the left in the late 1930s are Taylor's stores and on the right is McKee Motor Company, a Ford dealership operated by the Casteel Family. (Courtesy of Jack Norris)

Pictured in front of Taylor's Furniture and Hardware Store in 1955 are Martha Day Taylor and her daughter-in-law, Loretta Taylor. (Courtesy of Fern Morgan)

Above: Jack Norris took this picture in 1987, just before these stores behind Campbell's Drugstore were demolished. These once housed a restaurant, grocery, furniture store, and a tavern. The upper floors were probably dwellings. The small building on the right was John Llewellyn's law office. The Llewellyn home, which still stands, can barely be seen on the left above the roof line of the stores.

Right: Charlie Norris and nephew, Jack Norris, are pictured here, about 1941, on the courthouse lawn. The businesses on Water Street behind them are Norris' Grocery on the left, with the Leonard Moore store next to it; and in the small building on the right is Ned Johnson's barber shop. The corner of Collin's Furniture Store can be seen on the far right. (Courtesy of Jack Norris)

THE WHITE HOUSE CLINIC

■ ■ ■

The White House Clinic was opened by Dr. Phillip Curd in 1973 in McKee. The staff in 1974 were: Barry Curry, dentist, Kathy Rose (later Smith), Terrie Curd, Sylvia Moore, Bill Moore, and Ida Lakes. (Courtesy of Phillip Curd)

With the help of a philanthropist from Ohio and the Jackson County Bank, Phillip Curd, a young physician fresh out of the Peace Corps, purchased from Earl Gabbard in 1973 a small, white house in McKee. Here, he established a medical practice, which in twenty-five years has grown from two doctors and a dentist in a little white house in McKee to three doctors and two dentists in a large stone building in McKee. Since then, three new clinics in Berea and Richmond have been opened. The White House Clinic is a nonprofit organization, governed by a board of directors which reflects the clinics' clientele. As a Federally Qualified Health Care Center, the Clinic receives federal funds to offset costs for uninsured and low-income patients.

Dr. Phillip Curd, who established the White House Clinic in 1973, is shown here in front of the new clinic, which opened in 1999. (Courtesy of Phillip Curd)

Contributing to this renaissance was not only the general prosperity of the 1990s, but also the designation of Jackson County as a federal Empowerment Zone in 1994. In order to achieve this designation, the citizens of Jackson County, under the leadership of County Judge-Executive William Smith and Kentucky Highlands Investment Corporation, came together in numerous public meetings to develop a strategic plan for economic growth. Their efforts were successful, and Jackson, along with Clinton and Wayne Counties, became part of a federal Empowerment Zone—one of only three in the United States. This designation, due to expire in 2009, brought with it various tax incentives designed to encourage economic development and redevelopment.

Top left: These buildings, at the corner of Main and First (Gotfrey) Streets, housed various enterprises over the years. They were incorporated into the Jackson County Bank building in 1990. (Courtesy of Jack Norris)

Top right: A new facelift to these buildings on Second Street in McKee gives a new look to downtown in 2007. (Photograph by Jean Fee)

Above: The new Jackson County Public Library, opened in 2006, stands on land once occupied by Alfred Taylor's stores. (Photograph by Jean Fee)

The Empowerment Zone status also brought with it a federal grant for downtown revitalization and beautification. With matching funds from the state, the City of McKee, under Mayor Dwight Bishop, was able to replace and extend sidewalks, install new decorative street lights in the city-core, build a new police and fire headquarters, and purchase new equipment.

The expansion continues. Completed in 2007 was a new operations building for the telephone cooperative (PRTC), and, in 2009, a new Justice Center should be completed. This building will occupy the old Holcomb property at the corner of First (earlier Gotfrey) and Main Streets.

ANNVILLE
Annville, once known as Chinquapin Rough, originated as a quaint village in the southwestern area of Jackson County. Almost ten miles away from the county seat, McKee, it was a relatively quiet agricultural community.

Growing abundantly on the hills that interrupted the landscape was a rather small, angular bush which bore chestnut-like pods. This chinquapin was so well-known and attractive that its name was taken for the local post office—first opened in 1878. Several years later, the name was changed to Annville.

E. W. Johnson, a local businessman and farmer, was appointed postmaster sometime around 1890. It was he who was able to get the name of the post office changed to Annville in honor of his wife, Nancy Ann Johnson. Since his early tenure as postmaster, that position has been held by numerous others. And with the growth of Annville, a new post office has been constructed.

In its early days, Annville was little more than a place name; but over the years, several business enterprises and local cultural institutions made their stamp on the life of this area. This tight-knit little town has fostered a surprising and significant number of important concerns.

Herbert Morgan's store in Annville, once located where the Town and Country Market is today, carried a large variety of dry goods and agricultural supplies. In the 1960s, ice cream cones available here were a treat on hot summer days. (Courtesy of Ora Banks)

Annville Institute, which is named and discussed elsewhere in this book, was highly influential in the life and education of Jackson County citizens. Its location in Annville has naturally drawn attention and visitors to this area.

This picture, taken in the 1920s, shows the home of pharmacist and sometime-doctor, Dave Smith. The house still stands in Annville at its original location across from the Russell Hays Branch Bank. Dave Smith, though not a licensed physician, was a widely-known and respected healer in an area where few doctors practiced. (Courtesy of Mary Moore)

Hobert Banks' store (the building is still standing in Annville) was a small mercantile where locals met to sip cold drinks from the Coca-Cola box, gossip, and swap knives. Men and boys could get a haircut for fifty cents. (Courtesy of Ora Banks)

Shown above is a paving project undertaken in the early days of the Carpenter Trucking Company, which was established by Mib Carpenter. Over the years, this company grew to do major jobs and hauling all over the state and beyond. (Courtesy of Glenna Carpenter)

Its far-reaching effects can also be seen in that some who were educated there have been led to establish businesses in the Annville area as a kind of tribute to the considerable influence that was exerted upon their lives by the school and its leaders.

Of note was the establishment of Mid-South Industries at Annville in 1985. Its founder, Jerry Weaver, was an alumnus of Annville Institute and turned to Annville when looking for a new location for his business. The establishment of the Jackson County Regional Industrial Park at Annville has led to expanded employment opportunities, locally and regionally.

The town in the year 2007 is a far cry from the staid little village of yesterday. Important and growing businesses and community-service facilities of various kinds are located here. A modern medical clinic and pharmacy provide excellent services to an area that once had few medical professionals. An excellent nursing and rehabilitation center is also part of this. The Annville Institute campus still houses a mission outreach of the Reformed Church in America, the Jackson County Ministries; and the Barnabas Home for children also is located on the old campus.

Numerous groceries, garages, electronics and television works, and a major trucking company (Carpenter's Trucking) serve the community with not only goods and services but also with employment opportunities. Among the local service organizations is also an excellent and up-to-date fire department.

The Jackson Manor, built in 1989, is a sixty-one-bed facility for long-term nursing care. This is the only facility of its kind in the county. (Photograph by Jean Fee)

ANNVILLE MEDICAL CLINIC

■ ■ ■

The return of David Hays to the small, rural county of his birth, after finishing medical school, serves as an example of true community spirit. When he opened a small medical clinic in Annville in July of 1980, one wonders if Dr. Hays envisioned the success and expansion that would occur. Over the years, he has been able to open four additional clinics: East Bernstadt in 1982, London-Corbin in 1989, Burning Springs in 1998, and McKee in 2002. And in 2007, eight providers serve these clinics.

The Annville Medical Clinic was established in 1980 by Dr. David Hays. Pictured here on the steps of the first clinic are Doctors Hays and Ulrich, in the center, with their parents, Ed and Lucille Hays on the left and Mr. and Mrs. Ulrich on the right. (Courtesy of Violet Allen)

Annville, in 2007, is a thriving and progressive community. The years have brought it positive growth and a more diverse population. It proudly takes its place among its sister neighborhoods throughout the county as a productive and vibrant entity.

SAND GAP

Perched high on a ridge with a wide ranging vista, Sand Gap was first known as Collinsworth. Its first post office was established in 1886, with William N. Hurst as postmaster. The name was changed to Sand Gap in 1902.

This small community was, in its early days, a center for the exchange of goods and was a way station for drovers on their way to Richmond and its markets. In a 2007 interview, Vades Dean, whose father, James A. (Jim) Johnson, ran a general store in the 1920s and 30s, remembered that Sand Gap was very small with a couple of stores and a grist mill:

> People mostly lived out on the ridges and hollows and would bring their corn to be ground into meal, and Cleve Hurst would take out so much corn in exchange for grinding. People would also bring their eggs and chickens

Carl Flinchum's electronics shop was among the very earliest to bring modern technology to local residents. Pick up services were available to bring in your television set or radio for repair. The business was later handed down to Carl's son, Steve, whose daughter, Jessica, is pictured here. (Courtesy of Jessica Flinchum)

This aerial view of Sand Gap, taken in the 1960s, shows the Sand Gap Elementary School in the background, with U.S. Highway 421 running through the town from the right and trailing off to the left as it heads toward McKee. (Courtesy of Jess Wilson)

to Sand Gap, where Tal Martin and Delbert Marcum would buy their chickens and eggs and take them to market. Drovers would come through with cattle and sheep—drivin' them to market in Richmond.

Jim Johnson's store, which was located just off U.S. 421 on what is now State Highway 2004, also housed the post office (he was the postmaster) and served as a dental office (he was also the "toothpuller"). Mrs. Dean recalled: "If us children saw someone coming down the road holding their jaw, we would run away quick, 'cause we knew they would soon be screaming."

Sand Gap reached its heyday in the 1930s and 1940s, when several large coal mines operated. The opening of mines brought people looking for work in a depressed economy. Coal camps grew up near the mines, sometimes with their own hotels and shanty towns. (Chapter 8 describes in more detail the coal industry in Jackson County.)

Top: Pictured here is Sand Gap as it looked in the 1950s. (Courtesy of Paul Rose)

Middle left: Pryse Venable is pictured here in front of his Garage and Body Shop in Sand Gap about 1958. (Courtesy of Beulah Venable)

Middle right: Sherman Reece and Carl Williams are pictured here on the porch of the B. T. Standafer home in Sand Gap in 1969. Later erected on this site was a memorial to the five Standafer brothers who served in World War II: Douglas, Ben T., Biff, Jack, and Massie. (Courtesy of Alice Harrison Reece)

Left: The Frosty-ette in Sand Gap stands today just as it was in the 1950s. Operated by Carol Sparks Carrier and her family for many years, it was the first drive-in in the county. (Courtesy of Carolyn York)

And Sand Gap boomed—there were boarding houses, stores, restaurants, a tavern and pool hall, a large commissary, and even a movie theater. Virgil Rose remembers it in the late 1930s: "People went out all the time, people all crowded up together; it was where the miners went after work and it was where they got paid. But when the mines went to closing, then I guess Sand Gap went to closing."

Pictured here is the John and Arlie Blair House in Gray Hawk—once a Methodist Church. Note the entrance on the gable end and the rather elaborate window upstairs. It was located on Gray Hawk Lane where the Rodney Morris home now stands. (Courtesy of JoAnne Moore)

Today it is hard to imagine the boom town that must have been Sand Gap. The Gap today is a sleepy crossroads, but still an important commercial and social center with post office, churches, restaurant, stores, and a branch bank.

GRAY HAWK

There are several stories about the naming of this small community. Some say it was named for an Indian chief who died there, and others say it got its name because a large number of chicken hawks became a nuisance and were killed there. Robert Rennick, in his 1975 survey of local post offices, says that it was named for two men: Gray and Hawk, who supposedly owned large tracts of land here. However it

Pictured here at their home in Gray Hawk in 1915 are Anse and Mary Hunter and children: Lillie, Addie, Eliza, and John. The core of this house has been incorporated into a modern one-story home on Gray Hawk Lane. (From the Anna Blair Collection, courtesy of JoAnne Moore)

was named, Gray Hawk appears to have been an early community, with a post office established in 1853. The first postmaster was John L. Hamilton.

This picturesque community sits in the rolling, upland meadows of southern Jackson County. This is farming country, and Gray Hawk was a center for collecting mail and buying the goods the farmers couldn't provide themselves. In the early 1900s, the Reformed Church in America established a school, church, and hospital in Gray Hawk. The Mary Isabelle Allen Hospital, built in 1913 by the Reverend Arthur Allen in memory of his sister, was a fourteen-bed facility with an operating room and emergency room. It was staffed by Dr. Georgiana De Jong and missionary nurses. Isaac Bowles, in his 1918 monograph, *History of Jackson County, Kentucky*, notes that, in 1917, the hospital handled 1,889 dispensary cases, 317 calls, 33 operations and 44 patients.

The hospital closed in 1927 and was transformed into a school. The second story of the hospital was removed and the building made into a four-room school. This school replaced an earlier church school, which was then converted into a church building for the Gray Hawk Reformed Church. The materials garnered from removing the second story of the hospital were used to build a manse for the church pastor.

At one time, Gray Hawk had three large general stores (Montgomery's, Robinson's, and Spurlock's), an automobile garage and dealership owned by Everett and Jim King, and two sawmills.

Today, Gray Hawk is home to Gray Hawk Building Supply, which occupies the old King Motor Company building, D & W Electrical Supply, Jackson County Head Start, several small groceries, filling stations, and restaurants, two churches, and the only veterinary clinic in the county.

Top left: The Mary Isabelle Allen Hospital was a fourteen-bed facility built in Gray Hawk in 1913. It was the first and only hospital in Jackson County. In 1927, it was remodeled to became the Gray Hawk Community School. This building is no longer standing. (From the Fred De Jong Collection, courtesy of the De Jong family)

Top right: The L. J. Robinson store building still stands in Gray Hawk, looking much as it did years ago. It was one of three large general stores in the area, including Montgomery's and Spurlock's. (Courtesy of JoAnne Moore)

Above: The community of Gray Hawk in 2007 is home to the Gray Hawk Building Supply, pictured in the center, with D & W Electrical Supply to the right. (Photograph by Jean Fee)

The Tyner Garage and Grocery, shown here in 1973, did a brisk business at the crossroads of Highways 30 and 421. It was run originally by the Reynolds Family, then Boyd York, and then David Parrett. Later Burley Pennington took over, and finally Curt Seals. The building still stands, having been remodeled into apartments. (Courtesy of Eddie and Patsy Miller)

TYNER

Tyner, like Sand Gap, was and is a crossroads community. It is located where State Highway 30 and U.S. Highway 421 intersect—a natural place for development. By 1880, a post office had been established and Tyner was on the map.

Amos Miller, pictured here in 1940, ran a garage in Tyner for many years—interrupted only by service in World War II. (Courtesy of Eddie and Patsy Miller)

Paul Jones recalls that Tyner had several businesses in the 1940s. He recalls an automobile garage, a wholesale grocery business, and an automobile dealership. The dealership, opened by the W. R. Reynolds family after World War II, sold Chryslers, Plymouths, and, later, International Harvester tractors. Paul Jones bought the company in 1956 but closed it after a year. Mr. Jones recalls that "it just wasn't feasible anymore because transportation was better and people could go to London and Richmond to shop."

In 1936, the WPA began the construction of a gymnasium to serve the existing Tyner School, which then housed all twelve grades. However, the new building was severely damaged by fire before its completion. It was then renovated for use as a high school. These schools are closed now, and Flat Rock Furniture Manufacturing occupies the school campus.

Of importance to the entire county was the construction of Beulah Lake at Tyner in the late 1960s. Sometimes called Tyner Lake, this is the source of drinking water for most county residents. The Jackson County Water Association was established in 1969 to build a water treatment and supply system, and the first treatment plant and water lines were completed in 1973, serving 518 customers. Today, with a new treatment plant completed in 2005, the Association serves 4,500 customers. This lake has also fostered residential growth near the lake.

Tyner today remains a viable crossroads community, with post office, church, grocery and gasoline store, and tractor and mower repair shop. Nearby, between Tyner and Gray Hawk is the site of the annual "Stringbean" Memorial Bluegrass Music Festival.

Tyner today is a busy crossroads. The building on the left once housed the Tyner Post Office until it moved into the brick building on the right. (Photograph by Jean Fee)

Fred De Jong took this picture of Gray Hawk Reformed Church in 1924. (Courtesy of the De Jong family)

Churches

*T*he people who migrated from the American colonies into the Appalachian Mountains were largely descendants of Scotch-Irish, English, and German Protestants, looking for religious freedom from the state churches of Europe. The characteristics which inspired these people to seek land in hostile places—independence, self-reliance, tenacity, a passion for self-determination—also drove their religious faith. They brought with them a faith seasoned in Calvinism and a strong belief in democratic equality and the priesthood of all believers. (Shapiro, 1978) (McCauley, 1995)

In the very early days of settlement on the frontier, worship services would be held in homes until the communities became more established. Services might be conducted by circuit riders, many of whom came into the mountains with the settlers. Later on, log "meetin" houses would be built, usually on land donated by an organizer. As the area developed with sawmills to cut weatherboard, the log structures were covered with weatherboard and whitewashed.

Until the closing of many of the one-room schoolhouses in the county, communities used the same building for various functions: public school during the week, church services on Sunday, and, on occasion, for social events, such as pie suppers. It was more likely the consolidation of schools, not the 1960s Supreme Court ruling on separation of church and state, which changed this in our county.

Circuit riders were probably the earliest missionaries of frontier times, riding from community to community, preaching in homes and tents. The Reverend William Anderson, a Baptist Circuit Rider of the late 1800s, was also the first pastor of Oak Grove Baptist Church, serving from 1889–1930. (Courtesy of Ramona Jones)

The Reverend Fayette Powell stands in front of the Chestnut Flat School house, which also served as a meeting house for the Chestnut Flat Pentecostal Church. He preached here in the 1940s and 50s, when the use of school buildings for church and community meetings was common practice. (Courtesy of Nolan Powell)

The Methodist circuit riders were active in Kentucky very early, and it is likely that they frequented the Jackson County area long before there were established churches. However, it was the Baptists who established the first churches in what was to become Jackson County. The Christian denomination followed soon. Later came the Pentecostal/Holiness, and Reformed Churches. And lastly, the Catholic Church was established. Following is a brief history of the tenure of these denominations in the county.

The Baptist Church

Before the formation of Jackson County in 1858, several Baptist Churches were active in the area. They included the Clover Bottom Church, established sometime prior to 1842, Mt. Gilead, established in 1844, and White

Springs, established in 1853. A brief, handwritten note found in records collected by Mrs. June Sasser, wife of Pastor Jim Sasser (now deceased), mentions a Flat Lick Church established in 1849. Available records show no other churches active until the Civil War era, when the Sand Gap (1860), Union (1862), Pond Creek (1866), and Annville (1866) churches were formed.

Following is a look at a few of these historic churches. The names of church officers and members noted below are spelled as they appear in the transcribed records.

Clover Bottom Baptist Church

The first church of record in what was to become Jackson County was the Clover Bottom Baptist Church, which was organized by Joseph Ambrose sometime prior to 1842, when the first records are available. Sent by the General Association of Baptists in Kentucky, Mr. Ambrose was also instrumental in the founding of the churches of White Springs and Mt. Gilead.

Church records from 1842 until about 1845 refer to Clover Bottom as a "Regular Baptist Church of Christ at Clover Bottom." The following are listed as members: Joseph Ambrose, pastor; John B. Harrison, clerk; Rachel Baker; John Balanger; Aaron Powell; and Rachel Van Winkle. Records indicate that by 1845 the name had been changed to the "United Baptist Church of Christ at Clover Bottom." In this year, the following were ordained as deacons: Joseph Ambrose, John Ward, Charles Witt, John B. Harrison, Burgess Baker, Luis Baker. And Polly Baker and Pagia Davis were ordained as "deaconess with husband." Later, the church was incorporated as the Clover Bottom Missionary Baptist Church.

The first Clover Bottom Church building was a log structure, which in 1902 was replaced by a frame building. The logs from the first church building were either sold or donated to Berea College, where they stand now as a residence. The Clover Bottom

Clover Bottom Baptist Church, the oldest church in the county, was established about 1841. The first building was of logs and stood very near the current building, which is pictured here. The logs from the first church building now reside in Berea as part of a private residence. (Photograph by Fletcher Gabbard)

Baptist Church, having undergone several building changes since 1842, is the longest continuously active church in Jackson County.

In a publication celebrating the thirtieth Homecoming, there is the following:

> Several local churches can trace their origins to Clover Bottom Missionary Baptist Church. The first of these was the White Springs Baptist Church in 1853. The next church was Sand Gap Baptist Church in 1860. The Big Hill Baptist Church was first organized in 1924 with assistance from the Clover Bottom Baptist Church. Evidently, this church died out after a few years. In 1951 a new Big Hill Baptist Church was constituted and organized through the leadership of Brother Charlie Lunsford and others from Clover Bottom Missionary Baptist Church. In 1960, the church assisted with the constituting and organization of the Deer Stable Missionary Baptist Church. In 1989, the church agreed to be the Mother church for the constituting and organization of the Old Orchard Missionary Baptist Church. (From the papers of Anna Lunsford Rose, n.d., courtesy of Flora Richardson.)

Mt. Gilead Baptist Church

Mt. Gilead United Baptist Church of Christ at Tyner was organized by Joseph Ambrose and John Ward in 1844. Like Ambrose, Ward had also been appointed a missionary by the General Association of Baptists in Kentucky and was active in the establishment of several churches in the county.

Mount Gilead Baptist Church, established in 1844, was a six-sided log structure. This 1904 picture of the Irvine Association at Mt. Gilead shows the church after it had been covered with weatherboarding. A new church building was built in 1908 and another in 2003. (Courtesy of June Sasser)

The first Mt. Gilead Church was a log building built on land owned by John Ward "by Sturgeon Creek at the mouth of Double Lick Branch." It was a six-sided structure, with a hole in the center of the roof, through which smoke could escape from the fire built in the large kettle in the middle of the room during cold weather. Seats were made of split logs and arranged on four sides of the kettle, and the pulpit occupied the corner of the other two sides.

A new structure, built in 1908 on land donated by Albert G. Ward, served as the church building for many years, although it was remodeled several times. A new building was constructed on the property in 2003 and the old structure removed. Mount Gilead was affiliated with the South Fork Association until about 1862, when this Association was dissolved. It then joined the Irvine Association. In 1925, Mt. Gilead was one of the churches that helped to organize the Jackson County Association of Missionary Baptists. In 1968, the Church voted not to be affiliated with any organization.

Annville Baptist Church

According to church records transcribed by June Sasser, the Chinquapin Rough Baptist Church was "constituted as an 'arm' from Mt. Gilead Baptist Church" in 1866. The "arm" consisted of thirteen members from that church: McChager Cope, Mary Cope, Sarah York, Redman Trewet, Elizabeth Trewet, G. W. King, Tobitha King, G. W. Cook, Melvina Cook, Howel Brewer, Polly Ann Brewer, Joel Coffee, and Nancy Arnold. The first pastor was John Ward, and the church clerk was G. W. King. McChager Cope and G. W. Cook were deacons.

Other documents state that the Chinquapin church was organized by Andrew Isaacs and Alex Robbins and first met in the home of McChager and Pollie Cope. The first church building was of log on land belonging to the Cope family. Later, they donated the land to the church. A larger frame building was erected in 1913, with the church using the downstairs, and the Masonic Lodge the upstairs.

McChager Cope, one of the founders of the Chinquapin Rough Baptist Church (later Annville Baptist Church) in 1866, is shown here with his daughters. The church first met in Cope's home, probably the building pictured here. Outdoor photography in the 1860s was a complicated procedure, and a picture from this era is a real treasure. (Courtesy of George Roach)

In 1932, the name of the church was changed to Annville Missionary Baptist Church. And, in 1956, the present church was built, but has undergone several renovations since then.

Union Baptist Church

Records collected by June Sasser state that the Union Baptist Church first met in 1862 with William Stannifer serving as moderator and Abner Holcomb as clerk. Later records state that Union was organized in 1869 at the home of Abner Holcomb. Early ministers included A. D. Collins, B. F. Lamb, and Elias Fletcher.

Other Baptist Churches

Between 1873 and 1900, at least eight additional Baptist Churches were organized, including Grassy Springs (1873), Birch Lick (1874), Green Hill (1876), Friendship (1886), Kerby Knob (1887), Oak Grove (1889), Wind Cave (1894), and New Zion (1895). (There may have been an earlier Friendship Church. The Laurel River Association minutes of 1884 mention a Friendship Church in Jackson County in 1860.)

From 1910 to 1934, at least eleven additional Baptist Churches were founded, including Owsley Fork in 1909, Maulden in 1910, Pilgrim's Rest in 1913, Egypt in 1914, Gray Hawk in 1914, Mt. Zion in 1922, Blackwater #1 in 1922, Bond in 1922, Big Hill (1924 and 1951), Tyner in 1930, and Bethel in 1934.

The *Proceedings of the Fiftieth Session of the Irvine Association, Missionary Baptists of Kentucky, 1909* lists several early churches for which there are no

Getting to and from church was a cold affair in the wintertime of the 1920s. Pictured here is the Jim Brumback family returning from church. (Courtesy of Ramona Jones)

It would appear that hanging out the window was more fun than posing for the Sunday School (or perhaps Bible School) picture. Shown here are the children of Oak Grove Baptist Church in 1924. (Courtesy of Ramona Jones)

Top: The Egypt Baptist Church was established in 1914 in the Jackson County Baptist Institute Church building, shown here on "Happy Top." The building was moved closer to the road in 1937 where it functioned until 1968, when it was replaced with a new structure. (Courtesy of Jess Wilson)

Left top: Gray Hawk Baptist Church was established as an arm of the Oak Grove Church in 1914. This is a picture of the first church building, no longer standing. (From the Anna Blair Collection, courtesy of JoAnne Moore)

Left bottom: Ervin and Martha Privett, shown here, donated the land for the Gray Hawk Baptist Church. (From the Anna Blair Collection, courtesy of JoAnne Moore)

Right: Pictured here is the Wind Cave community gathered together to witness and celebrate the hanging of the bell in 1924. The Wind Cave Baptist Church was established in 1894. (Courtesy of Regina Brewer)

One of the largest baptizings in the county was held by the Bond Baptist Church in 1925. The Reverend A. C. Cornelius is officiating. He had been a previous pastor at Bond and returned for this revival. (Courtesy of the Jackson County Public Library)

founding dates and so are not listed above. However, we know they were here before 1909. They are Liberty, Indian Creek, and Drip Rock.

Shown here in 1953 is the McKee Baptist Church, which was organized in 1940. A new church building was constructed and dedicated in 1957. (Courtesy of Paul Sears)

More recent times have seen the founding of the McKee Baptist Church in 1940, Letterbox in 1940, Deer Stables in 1961, Old Orchard in 1988, and Pine Grove (exact date unknown.)

The scope of this book does not permit a more detailed look at the history of the many Baptist Churches in the county. And the lack of available records has no doubt led to the omission of many from the list above. Suffice it to say that the history of the Baptist denomination in Jackson County is long and prolific. In 2007, forty-four Baptist churches were listed in *The Jackson County Sun,* with most of the early churches still in existence.

THE METHODIST CHURCH

At the writing of this book there is one Methodist Church in the county: the Annville United Methodist Church, established in 1994. However, that is not to say that the Methodists had not been active in the county in earlier times. In an unpublished manuscript entitled, *History of Early Jackson*

County, June Sasser states: "The Methodists had an active ministry in the county very early and two Methodist ministers resided in Jackson County in 1860." A note in the Anna Blair Collection of pictures indicates that her family's home in Gray Hawk was once a Methodist Church.

The Methodist circuit riders were well-known on the frontier, many times following close behind the settlers in their westward movement. In the September 2007, issue of *The Kentucky Explorer*, an article describes these fearless men:

> These men riding horseback around a chain of appointments, which required four to six weeks to complete and which varied in length up to one thousand miles, efficiently adapted themselves to the crude frontier conditions. The earliest preachers lived in the homes of the people and had no such physical aids as missionary societies, Sunday School societies, church papers, or Bible or Tract societies. ... They must have been men of intense zeal and religious conviction, considering the hardships they underwent. (p.46)

Robert Bingham was a circuit rider for the Methodist Church, traveling and preaching widely throughout the mountains of southeastern Kentucky from about 1840 to 1890. In his later years, he built a log church at Buncomb Creek in Jackson County. (Lawson, 1996)

The Annville United Methodist Church had its roots in a small Bible study group meeting in homes in the Annville-Tyner area in 1992, and, in 1994, the church was formally established. Charter members were Edith and Roy

Annville United Methodist Church, established in 1992, had its roots in a small Bible study group meeting in homes. Pictured here is the church building in 2007. (Photograph by Fletcher Gabbard)

Top left: Cave Springs Christian Church, looking much as it did in the 1800s, still stands on Cave Springs Road. It is the oldest Christian Church in the county, and services have been held continually since the 1860s. (Courtesy of Wanda Renner)

Top right: The Cornett's Chapel Christian Church congregation is shown here in 1917. Founded in 1908, the church closed its doors in 1970. (Courtesy of Mary Moore)

Above: The Sand Gap Christian Church is pictured here as it stood in the 1950s on Highway 2004. The church moved to the Deer Stables in 1973, and the building pictured above now houses an antique store. (Courtesy of Bessie Adams)

Collett, Charles, Alma, and Susan Kilburn, Ted, Martha, Heather, and Gina Hays, Naomi Quiggins, Rita Collett, Joseph Collett, Sandra Madden, Judy Collett, Don Roy Collett, and Robert Shinevarre.

THE CHRISTIAN CHURCH

According to Mrs. Sasser, the Christian denomination had a very early church near Clover Bottom—probably in the 1860s. It is believed that this was the Cave Springs Christian Church. Minnie Van Winkle, whose husband, James Leslie, preached in the Christian Churches in Clay and Jackson Counties in the 1940s and 1950s, remembers hearing that the Cave Springs Church was "the oldest Christian Church this side of the Blue Ridge Mountains."

Cornett's Chapel Christian Church was organized around the year 1908, and a building was erected on land donated by John Cornett of Moores Creek. The first pastor was Henry Lewis. Early church members included the Henry Lewis family, George Freeman family, A. J. Johnson family, John Cornett family, Preston Eversole family, James Harvey Thomas family, McCowan family, and Jake Lakes family. The church had an active membership for many years; but with dwindling membership, Cornett's Chapel closed its doors in 1970.

The Sand Gap Christian Church, established in 1911, first occupied a church building on U.S. Highway 421 where the Sand Gap Holiness Church now meets. A new building was constructed on Highway 2004—not far from the original building. Then, in 1973, the church moved to the Deer Stables, where it is now housed in an even newer and larger building.

Christian churches still active in the county in 2007 include Cave Springs, Conway, Sand Gap, and Three Links Christian Churches. Two Christian Churches closely associated with the county, but just over the county line, are Mt. Olivet (established 1884 on Terrell's Creek and later relocated in 1919) and McWhorter (established 1893).

THE PENTECOSTAL AND HOLINESS CHURCHES

In his book, *The Flight of the Dove*, Alfred Carrier states that the Pentecostal doctrine was brought to Jackson County by the Reverend John Blackburn about 1908. Reverend Blackburn had been a Methodist minister and the presiding Elder of the Rockcastle Circuit in 1906. He apparently embraced the Pentecostal faith about 1907. Meetings were first held in an old store building at Letterbox, and, in 1910, a church was built. In 1916, this church was torn down, and the congregation established itself at Seven Pines.

Another early Pentecostal Church was at Moores Creek, probably established about 1908 on land donated by Alfred Wilson. This information was given to Carrier in an interview with Pearl Wilson Boggs, daughter of Mr. Wilson. Other interviews established that the Reverend Henry Dyche was leading the church on Moores Creek in 1919.

The Bond Holiness Church drew a large crowd during the 1950s. Vehicles line Highway 30 as far as the eye can see. (Courtesy of Opal Parrett)

Since these early beginnings, the Holiness and Pentecostal movement has continued in Jackson County. *The Jackson County Sun* listed twenty-eight Holiness and Pentecostal Churches within the county in 2007.

THE REFORMED CHURCH

The work of the Reformed Church in Jackson County began in 1900, when the Reformed Church in America sent two ladies, Mrs. Cora Smith of New York, a Bible teacher and registered nurse, and Miss Nora Gaut of Iowa, a Bible teacher, to start a school. These ladies first purchased a large cottage, which eventually became the parsonage, and began the construction of a school. By 1904, the McKee Academy, a school for grades one through eight, was complete; in 1907, the high school grades were added.

The McKee Reformed Church was organized in 1905, and, during the early years, church services were held in the school building. The first pastor was the Reverend Isaac Messler, who arrived in McKee with his wife and daughter in May of 1905.

The McKee Reformed Church, founded in 1905, is shown here in the 1920s. The church building underwent extensive remodeling in the 1950s. Shown here next to the church is the McKee Academy, which no longer stands. (Courtesy of Jess Wilson)

Reverend Messler states in a letter home:

> Frank Hull Wright and Mrs. John S. Allen assisted me in a series of meetings and we organized with twenty-seven members. Preaching services were held in the Academy. The church membership grew steadily. Mrs. Jos. S. Bussing donated money for a building in memory of her husband. I started the building but left [1918] before it was completed. Mr. De Jong, my successor in McKee, has drawn to the church the very best elements in the village and the organization is strong and efficient. (*Annville Institute, 1909–1978*, 1998. 6)

In 1906, mission work expanded to Gray Hawk, where, as in McKee, a school was established as the first priority. The Gray Hawk Community School, teaching grades one through eight, also served as the church on Sundays. Having served as a mission for twenty-two years, the Gray Hawk Reformed Church was officially organized in 1928. Charter members were Hugh K. Bennett, Janie L. Bennett, Robert N. Bennett, Effie Buss, Olivia Hays, James W. Hunter, Kate R. Hunter, John F. Hunter, Mattie S. Hunter, Ersie R. Judd, Harrison Parrett, Theresa Smallegan, and Ida Tanis.

In 1967, the church building was replaced with a modern structure on the site of the old church, and the present manse was completed in 1968. These buildings still stand.

Mission outreach in 1906 also included the building of a log school/church in the Adkins neighborhood on land purchased by a Miss Hoover of Elizabeth, New Jersey. By 1907, there was religious instruction at Smith, Sand Lick, Middle Fork, Gray Hawk, and Adkins. Services were held Sunday morning and evening at McKee and in the afternoon at one of the outlying areas.

Tanis Chapel was constructed on the Annville Institute campus in 1916 with funds provided by Richard Tanis and his family in memory of his wife. This church, although originally the chapel of Annville Institute, later became the Annville Reformed Church. A discussion of Annville Institute may be found in Chapter 5 of this book.

With the departure of Reverend Messler in 1918, the Reverend Fred De Jong became missionary

The Reverend Fred De Jong served as pastor of the McKee Reformed Church from 1918 to 1940. He is shown here with his wife, Betty, and children: Baby Beth, Gordon, and Carolyn. (Courtesy of James E. Hays)

Tanis Chapel, shown here soon after its completion in 1917, served as the chapel for the students at Annville Institute. Later it became known as the Annville Reformed Church, and stands today not much changed in appearance. (Courtesy of Jess Wilson)

pastor, first as a summer intern and later in a full-time capacity. He served twenty-two years before assuming the role of county-wide evangelist. Following the untimely death of Reverend De Jong in 1949, the Board of North American Missions of the Reformed Church in America chose Reverend Ray G. Hays to become the Evangelist-at-large for what became known as the Kentucky Mountain Work.

The specific assignment given to Reverend Hays included the formation of churches in the more remote regions of Jackson County and beyond. Over the course of more that forty-five years, Reverend Hays established Reformed Churches and highly active mission stations in eleven different locations. Chief among them were the churches at Sand Springs, Sinking Valley, Buncomb, and Cool Springs (Clay County). Sunday mission stations at Salt Rock, Pigeon Roost, Seven Pines, Terrells Creek, Powell, Hugg, Drip Rock, and Road Run were also started. These missions flourished for many years, but, in 1975, unable to sustain them, the Reformed Church in America closed them.

Jackson County Ministries
With the closing of Annville Institute in 1978, the Reformed Church established a missionary outreach program called the Jackson County Ministries (JCM). Housed on the Institute campus, JCM early on focused on providing

home repairs for the elderly and for low-income families. Many volunteers, then and now, participate in this program. At-risk youth was also an early focus, and JCM established various after-school and summer programs.

In the early 1990s, the emphasis on at-risk youth expanded, and a temporary shelter program for youth was established. This program was incorporated in 1993 as Barnabas Home, Inc. and has since expanded into a residential treatment program under contract with the State of Kentucky.

Although summer camps for the children of the county and housing repair programs continue, the Ministries has recently shifted its focus to serving the family as a whole, providing recreational activities in a Christian atmosphere. Particularly popular is a basketball intramural program for any and all, and the swimming pool is open to the public at scheduled times in the summer. A traveling puppet show, performed by young volunteers and staff, is much in demand at local churches.

Most recently, JCM, in conjunction with High Mountain Equine Outreach, is planning to provide a horseback-riding ministry for youth. This program should be up and running in 2008. Also located on the campus is the Annville Christian Academy, a private school (K-8) operated and controlled by parents.

The campus, and in particular the campground, is host to many retreats and is used by local churches as well as churches from as far away as Lexington.

THE CATHOLIC CHURCH

In 1950, the Roman Catholic Bishop of Covington, Bishop William Mulloy, designated a new mission territory in the Appalachian area and appointed

Father Ralph Beiting as the pastor in Garrard, Rockcastle, Jackson, and southern Madison Counties. In Jackson County, Father Beiting began his ministry with street preaching, and later held services in private homes. One of the first Catholic Church services in Jackson County was held in the home of Emma and Jack Moore near Tyner. In 1962, property in McKee was purchased, and a mobile home placed on the property for church services until a church building could be built. The first scheduled Catholic service was offered in McKee on May 6, 1962, with eight members in attendance in the mobile home.

The St. Paul Church building was completed and dedicated on July 14, 1963. After serious flood damage in June of 1981 and a second flood a few years later, the building was rebuilt, with major modifications and repairs, and rededicated in April 1992.

With the help of many volunteers, St. Paul Church early on established several outreach ministries—one of the earliest was to distribute used clothing, first through the church hall and then through The Attic store. A food pantry was begun where food was distributed to those in need—until the Jackson County Food Bank was organized in 1986. Revenues from the clothing store and donations were used for emergency assistance to pay for medicine, utilities, and rent when needed. The volunteers visit the handicapped and elderly throughout the county, sign up children for summer camp, and provide transportation to Camp Andrew Jackson. They also provided transportation to doctors' offices in London, Lexington, and Richmond until the Jackson County Transit was established.

St. Paul Catholic Church was established in McKee in 1962. The church building was dedicated in 1963. (Photograph by Jean Fee)

St. Paul Church hosts college, church, and high school groups to do home repairs and assist the elderly throughout the year. An annual Thanksgiving dinner is held for the elderly, and at Christmas the church hosts a Santa party during which the Nativity play is performed and Santa distributes toys and treats to all the children. In addition to the open Christmas party, toys and food vouchers are distributed to over one hundred families each year.

Christian Appalachian Project

Long before St. Paul Church was established at McKee, Father Beiting sought to address the needs of low-income people throughout his four-county parish. He called on his family and friends in Northern Kentucky for help, and, for several years, he made frequent trips to pick up food, clothing, and household goods to distribute to those in need.

Seeing the need to offer recreation and fellowship in a Christian atmosphere to needy children from the counties involved, the church purchased land on Sand Lick in Jackson County to build what became Camp Andrew Jackson. Here, children enjoy recreational and educational activities at day camp during the summer months, including a swim in the lake on the property.

Father Ralph Beiting, on the left, and Melvin Marks are pictured here in the 1960s going over plans for Camp Andrew Jackson. (Courtesy of Joyce Marks)

In 1964, these missionary efforts were incorporated as the nondenominational Christian Appalachian Project (CAP). Shortly thereafter, CAP began several business ventures in order to increase employment opportunities in Jackson County. These enterprises included a dairy farm established in 1964, a woodworking shop in 1967, a greenhouse in 1966, and, in 1968, a Christmas wreath factory and a sawmill. Most of these enterprises have since been purchased from CAP and continue as self-sustaining businesses in the county.

The Christmas wreath factory, which CAP operated until 1998, is no longer located in Jackson County, but continues under the auspices of the Mountain Economic Development Fund. The dairy farm was purchased by George Purcell and continues in operation today. The sawmill was purchased by Melvin Marks and continues. The woodworking venture, which operated for many years as Kentucky Woodcrafts, under the ownership of Kentucky Highlands Investment Corp., finally closed its doors in 2002. The greenhouse venture closed for a short time; then, in 1975, CAP's greenhouse manager, Dale Anastasi, returned to

Jackson County to open Anastasi's Greenhouses in Tyner. This enterprise now operates as Haverson's Family Farms.

Currently, much of CAP's emphasis includes the development of human potential, addressing long-term needs, such as family development centers, counseling services, tutoring, adult literacy programs, teen centers, life skills training, job training, and affordable housing. Programs addressing short-term needs include elderly visitation, emergency financial assistance, spouse-abuse shelters, a prescription assistance program, food and gift baskets at Christmas, respite for families whose members have disabilities, and instruction for parents in teaching pre-schoolers with disabilities.

Father Beiting, shown here in 2005, began his missionary work in Appalachia in 1950, building St. Paul Catholic Church in McKee, Kentucky, in 1963, and incorporating the Christian Appalachian Project in 1964. (Courtesy of Joyce Marks)

In 1986, CAP received a large donation of books which launched a program known as "Operation Sharing." Presently, many goods, including books, food, garden seeds, and home repair supplies are distributed to organizations in all of the Appalachian counties of Kentucky as well as Appalachian areas in twelve other states. Much of CAP's work is the result of its nearly one hundred volunteers. CAP also employs over three hundred people in full- and part-time positions, making CAP the largest private service organization in eastern Kentucky.

This "District School" in Gray Hawk may have been typical of the weather-boarded buildings which first replaced the very early log schools. (From the Fred De Jong Collection, courtesy of the De Jong family)

Schools

Fond Memories

*I*n the early days of settlement in the Appalachian Mountains, educational opportunities were very limited. Schooling at home or at "subscription schools" might be all that were available. Subscription schools might be established by teachers, who charged a fee to teach, or by parents to educate their own children and any neighbors who would help pay the teacher. In an obituary for "Franklin" (Alexander Frank) Hays in the June 6, 1924, edition of *The Berea Citizen,* there is a record of a subscription, or "select," school at Gray Hawk "kept by a Mr. Stewart" in 1850, and also one at Kerby Knob "kept" by J. W. Van Winkle in 1867. These schools were both attended by Alexander Frank Hays—at Gray Hawk when he was about ten years old and at Kerby Knob when he was twenty-seven. After returning from the Civil War, Hays tried his hand at farming in Gray Hawk and for a short time in Illinois but then joined his father, Robert, in farming at Kerby Knob. It was here that he felt the need to further his education and, at the advanced age of twenty-seven, entered school again. It was at Van Winkle's subscription school that Hays met his future wife, Wilmouth Frances Hudson.

Perhaps the Sparks School, which still stands on Bill's Branch about two miles north of McKee, was one of these early "pay" schools. Jeremiah Sparks, returning from the Civil War in 1863 and determined to see that his children had an education, built a log structure to be used exclusively as a school on his property. Although it is unclear when Mr. Sparks constructed the building, it is known that his oldest son would have been about six years old in

The Sparks School still stands on Bill's Branch, having been converted into a barn many years ago. Built by Jeremiah Sparks after his return from the Civil War, this is a prime example of the very earliest school buildings. (Photograph by Jean Fee)

1863, and it is known that a son, Isaac Kanada Sparks, born in 1869, went to school there. So this school could have been built any time after 1863 but before the early 1870s, when Isaac would have attended school there. This school building still stands on the original Sparks farm, having been incorporated into use as a barn. (Wilson, 1981)

This chapter looks at the rise of public education in Jackson County, tracing the evolution from the one-room schools of yesteryear to the consolidated schools of today. Beyond the subscription schools of the 1800s were other private schools, and these, too, are chronicled here.

COMMUNITY ONE-ROOM SCHOOLS

Kentucky's first system of free public education was created and passed by the Kentucky General Assembly on February 16, 1838. It provided for a state superintendent of public instruction and a state board of education, which appointed five trustees to run each school district. Today, board members (trustees) are elected by the public, instead of appointed.

By 1875, a nationwide interest in providing education for America's children had a firm hold. In rural areas, such as Jackson County, many children lived too far away to attend the town schools. Therefore, counties were divided into districts, and, in time, each district set up its own one-room schoolhouses. In these one-room schools, all grade levels met in a single room with a single teacher. The quality of facilities at one-room schools varied with local economic conditions, and, generally, the number of children at each grade level would vary with local populations.

Each school had five to eight levels of elementary-age students. The curriculum consisted of the "three R's, reading, riting and rithmetic." Many like to think they taught "five R's," the last two being "respect and responsibility." And a long hickory switch was sometimes seen at the schoolmaster's desk. This "enforcer," when called upon, would appear and yield the proper amount of discipline according to the degree of lack of respect.

Students desiring schooling beyond level eight had to attend boarding schools outside the county. Secondary education did not come to Jackson County until 1907, when the Reformed Church in America added high school grades to the McKee Academy.

The most active period of building public schools in Jackson County appears to have taken place during the 1890s, possibly because of the passage of the 1888 Common School Law, which provided funding for operating schools statewide. With the population increasing and transportation inadequate, it was necessary to construct numerous one-room schools, many within just a few miles of each other. (Hudson, 1996)

Students usually walked to school on a dirt road in all kinds of weather. Some of the homes were as much as one and one-half miles away from the schoolhouse and others farther. The first two months (July 10–September 10) of school were well attended. After September 10th, older children were sometimes kept home to help with chores and harvest the crops on family farms. In the winter months, the heavy rains and snows made it virtually impossible for children to walk this distance, and absenteeism was high. Nevertheless, Bowles reports that in 1919, the attendance rate for ten- to fourteen-year-olds was eighty-six percent, for fifteen- to seventeen-year-olds, sixty percent, and for eighteen- to twenty-year-olds the rate was twenty-six percent. (Bowles, ca. 1919, 10) This seems astounding when one considers that no truant officer was in place during this period, and the state law of compulsory attendance was seldom applied. Whether or not children attended school regularly depended entirely on the parents and sometimes the weather.

It is noteworthy to mention here a finding by Norman Frost that "...in 1910 there was a larger proportion of children enrolled in school in the Appalachian region than in the entire state in general." (Hudson, 1996, p. 101)

Baker School, located between Hisel and Kerby Knob, was typical of early one-room schoolhouses. (Courtesy of Ben Powell)

Teachers at these one-room schools usually boarded with a local family during the school year. In the winter months, they would get to school early to start a fire in the potbelly stove so the building would be warm when the students arrived. On many occasions, the teacher would prepare a hot noon meal on top of the potbelly stove. Otherwise, students brought their lunch from home in a four-pound lard bucket or in a brown paper bag. A typical "bag lunch" might consist of a biscuit with jam and butter, meat, beans, apples, fried potatoes, and boiled eggs.

A typical school day began when the bell sounded for "books" at 8 a.m. Each day began with the pledge to the flag and, on many occasions, the Lord's Prayer. School ended at 4 p.m., with students having had a morning and afternoon recess of fifteen minutes each and an hour for lunch. Games played during these breaks might include softball, tag, hide-n-seek, marbles,

This 1930s picture appears to have captured a school festival in progress at the Privett School, with parents and friends seated on the bank to watch performances by the students. (Courtesy of Mary Coffey)

hopscotch, horseshoes, farmer-in-the-dell, red rover, little-white-house-on-the-hill, jumping rope, and Annie-over. If available, a board would be placed across a tree stump to make a seesaw.

Older students were given responsibilities of bringing water in from a spring or a drilled well close to the school and carrying in the wood or coal used for heating the building. The younger students would be given responsibilities according to their size, age, and gender. Jobs might include taking the erasers outside for dusting, cleaning the blackboard, or sweeping the floor.

One of the highlights of the year was the annual "school fair." It was held at a different school each year for one school day, before winter began. The school fair consisted of contests between the schools in academics and athletics and dinner-on-the ground. School projects for this special day were displayed with several teachers serving as judges. Academic events included reading, writing, spelling bee, oration, math, science, and geography. Sport events might include softball throw, three-legged sack race, fifty-yard dash, seventy-five-yard dash, one hundred-yard dash, and relay races.

Events, such as "pie suppers," were organized to raise money for special events or for the purchase of additional school supplies. These pie suppers were usually a success because the ladies would bake the pies, and the gentlemen would bid on the pie belonging to their favorite girl. It was a fun social gathering for each small community.

TEACHER CERTIFICATION

In the early days, teachers were only required to take a certificate examination, given by commissioners, or a local doctor, who would then declare them eligible to teach. They could then later apply for their certificate. However, since 1872, teachers have been required to hold certificates before they could contract to teach at a school. The first Normal School for training teachers in eastern Kentucky was established in Jackson County in the 1890s by Professor Isaac Holcomb. According to a 1950s *Lexington Herald* article, Mr. Holcomb held "seven degrees ranging from law to penmanship." Classes were held in the front room on the second floor of the Holcomb family home at Maulden.

An article by Jess Wilson in the May, 1977, issue of *The Rural Kentuckian*, notes the existence of temporary training programs for teachers. One who qualified in this manner was Harvey Combs, of Annville, who taught at the Wind Cave School in 1892. Mr. Combs attended a week-long Teacher's Institute at McKee, August 15–19, 1892, qualifying as a teacher with a score of sixty-five percent on the examination. The Wind Cave School was a twenty-by-twenty-foot log building with no floor or fireplace, located near where the present-day Wind Cave Baptist Church sits. In Harvey's class that year there were twenty-six students, ages six to seventeen, enrolled for the five-month term.

Winter schools were common in the early 1900s—giving teachers a chance to improve their skills. Bob Bradshaw, superintendent of schools, conducted such a school in 1900. Mr. Bradshaw is pictured here in the center first row. The only other identified teacher is George Rader, father of Alpha Rader Hays, in the second row, far left. (Courtesy of Nell Hays Westbrook)

In 1900, school began in July and was out for the year just before Christmas. With school out, those teachers who wished or needed to improve their skills could attend "winter school." Robert (Bob) Bradshaw, superintendent of Jackson County Schools in 1900, was the instructor for the county's winter schools.

The emphasis on teacher training continued, and, in an article in the June 7, 1929, issue of the Louisville *Courier-Journal*, Superintendent Leonard Moore reported the following:

> The county schools employ seventy-nine teachers. Despite the financial difficulties of the board, the average salary was $75 a month.... Teachers now average four years of high school. At the close of the elementary

school year, most of them attend training schools and colleges. The small number of teachers who do not attend school are taking extension courses.

Over the years, teacher certification has become even more accountable. Today, a teacher must complete a four-year college program in education, pass state-required tests, and complete a one-year internship program with state requirements before receiving a teaching certificate. In order to keep their certificates active, teachers must complete a fifth-year program, or receive a Masters degree, within a ten-year time frame.

SCHOOLHOUSES OF "YESTER-YEARS" AND EARLY CONSOLIDATION

Isaac Bowles, in his *History of Jackson County, Kentucky*, describes the early schools in Jackson County. He cites as his source Mr. J. R. Durham of Sand Gap:

> When the county was formed, the school houses were built of logs, sometimes hewed sometimes unhewed. Each one had a big stone chimney with a wide fireplace. These fireplaces varied in width ranging from four to nine feet. Often the smoke from these filled the room, this making it very uncomfortable for the pupils who sat upon one-half of a split log in which was adjusted wooden pegs which supported it at a proper height. …The floor was made of logs six or eight feet long, about twelve inches in diameter, split in the middle…with the split side up, and several of these lying side by side made the rough floor surface. In some instances the boards forming the roof were held in place by stones as weights while in other cases the boards were fixed with wooden pegs. Many of these schools were known as "Frog Pond" schools because the pupils were allowed to study aloud. (Bowles, ca. 1919, 9)

The Adkins School, although built in 1906 by the Reformed Church, gives a sense of what the very early log schoolhouses were like. By 1899, most of the log schools had been replaced by frame buildings. (Courtesy of James Earl Hays)

In 1899, the Commissioner of the State Bureau of Agriculture reported:

> In Jackson County we have sixty-eight public schools, somewhat upon the plan of all others in the state, only we can boast of the best schoolhouses of any in the state, as per our population and wealth. (Hudson, 1996, 92)

The superintendent of public schools also reported that there were only two log schoolhouses still being used in the county in 1899. (Hudson, 1996, 98) One of these may have been the Jeremiah Sparks School, which is discussed earlier in this chapter. If so, it had by this time become part of the public school system. It is unclear where the other log school was in 1899. But there is a record of a log school built at Adkins by the Reformed Church in 1906.

The Cave Springs School is a good example of the evolving, one-room schoolhouse. Instead of one door in the gable end, this later form had two entrances; one for the boys and one for the girls. Shown here in 1915 are: back row, left to right: Ida Abney (teacher), Dovie Van Winkle, Jon Dean, Leonard Abrams, June Robinson, Ray Dean, Milas Wilds, Winfred Van Winkle, Silas Wilds, Ethel Abrams, Dora Abrams, Susie Robinson, and Minta Hays; next row down: Clara Van Winkle, Minta Abrams, Pearl Van Winkle, LaVada Wilds, Lillian Abrams, Lena Abrams, Stella Wilds, America Dean, Zella Dean, and Jim Robinson; third row down, seated: Leslie Van Winkle, Cephas Abrams, Robert Abrams, Charlie Abney, Lloyd Van Winkle, Clifford Dean, LaVelle Van Winkle, Lola Abney, Mafra Azbill, Ethel Van Winkle, Eula Van Winkle, Rushia Van Winkle, Kinus Van Winkle, James Sidney Van Winkle, Vester Azbill, and John Allen Lane; and front row: Brodie Robinson, Bert Van Winkle, Robert Abrams, Richard Gay, Elmer Robinson, Ruffie Abrams, Ollie Abrams, Babe Robinson, and Clarence Bowlin. (Courtesy of Wanda Renner)

The turn of the century saw a massive effort to further public education. Log schoolhouses were replaced with modern frame buildings. And, by 1918, there were seventy-five one-teacher schools in Jackson County—all "modern frame buildings." (Bowles, ca. 1919, 9) Bowles reports that Superintendent Melvin Holcomb erected new buildings in fifty percent of the school districts.

Most of the new schools appear to have followed a similar plan, a rectangular structure with a single entrance located in the center of the gable. The first major change in the form of the one-room school was the addition of two doors, so the boys and girls could have separate entrances. (The Cave Springs School, pictured above, is a good example of this style.) Later on, a single, recessed doorway was added to some schools. (See the Cavanaugh School.)

Around 1916, V. O. Gilbert, state superintendent of public instruction, suggested that all light should come from the left side of the classroom, with the windows grouped close together. (One wonders why the left side. Perhaps the ruling assumed that all students were right-handed, and the additional

The Sparks School near New Zion illustrates the efforts to provide more lighting in the schools, with the requirement of a bank of windows "on the left side of the building." Shown here in 1949 are children at recess. (Courtesy of Judy Wilson)

light provided by more windows would fall on desks without shadows.) Whether this ruling applied only to new schools or all schools is unknown, but many schools in the county had this feature. For example, Sparks School (not the Jeremiah Sparks School), pictured nearby, has a six-bay-wide window bank, while others had five. It might have depended on the size of the school.

On August 12, 1918, Jackson County opened the first session of "Moonlight School," meeting on Monday evenings for twenty-eight weeks. This was part of Governor A. O. Stanley's adult literacy program, which hoped to teach fifty thousand people in Kentucky to read and write. H. F. Minter was superintendent of schools at this time, and he and four teachers taught the Moonlight School Course. He taught at McKee, Lizzie Isaacs at Egypt, S.S. Wolfe at Annville, J. A. Farmer at Clover Bottom, and J. R. Durham at Sand Gap.

This picture of Cavanaugh School, sometimes known as Upper Foxtown School, shows a typical one-room schoolhouse of the 1920s and 30s, with a single recessed door. The children in this picture are: front row, seated, left to right, Ari Lainhart, Maynard Mays, Jean Lainhart, Herbert Lakes, Mary Gay, and Dovie Lainhart; second row, Vera Rader, Eudell Fox, Homer Mays, Lawrence Gay, Levi Cain, Jay Fox, and Forrest Gay; third row, Charlie Moore, Warren Fox, and John D. Cox. (Courtesy of Dallas Fox)

The 1920s saw the beginnings of consolidation in the county schools. In a Louisville *Courier-Journal* article, dated June 7, 1929, Jackson County Superintendent Leonard Moore reported that there were seventy-two public schools in the county, sixty-seven of which were one-teacher schools, four were two-teacher schools, and one was a four-teacher school. Moore reported further that twelve modern school buildings were recently built; among these were the four two-teacher schools and the one four-teacher school mentioned above. (It appears that some consolidation is taking place.) He also reported:

> This year we are building a modern one-teacher rural school and an additional room to the Tyner Consolidated School, in which we are establishing the first junior high school in the county. Another room is being built on the Jackson County High School Building, which now is being used for both grade and High School work. Our programme for the next year or two contemplates adding one or two more junior high schools.

(The Jackson County High School Building mentioned in the quotation above was housed in the old McKee Academy, which the Reformed Church turned over to the county school system about 1921. This building, located where the parking lot of the McKee Reformed Church is today, was to undergo several more name changes—becoming the McKee High School, when high school grades were added at Tyner about 1931, and finally becoming McKee Elementary, when a new high school was built on the hill overlooking McKee in 1938.)

PRIVATE SCHOOLS

The Jackson County Baptist Institute.

In 1892, the Irvine Association of Kentucky Baptists, in conjunction with the Booneville, Laurel River, Goose Rock, and other Associations, established a school of "higher learning" at Burning Springs called the Lorimer School. But, in 1907, the other Associations involved in this endeavor began to direct their attention to Oneida Baptist Institute, and the Irvine Association moved its work to Egypt, where they established the Baptist Institute on "Happy Top." (Later, the Egypt Missionary Baptist Church would be organized here.) June Sasser recounts the beginning of the

The girls' dormitory of the Jackson County Baptist Institute is shown here under construction at Oak Grove about 1926 or 1927. When completed, it housed twenty girls and several teachers. When the Institute closed in 1930, the building was sold and used first as a rental home and then as a tobacco barn. It was demolished in the early 1980s. (Courtesy of Sue and Larry Woolum)

Jackson County Baptist Institute in an unpublished manuscript entitled *History of Irvine Association of Kentucky Baptists*:

> This school was remarkably successful for several years, being one of the first schools of "Higher Learning" in the County. It was not a High School but took the students from the local schools at whatever grade level they were and helped them to prepare for college or to pass teacher's examinations or whatever they wished to prepare for. By 1925 the school seemed to be going down so the association moved it to Oak Grove.

The following excerpt is from a 1928 pamphlet (no author) seeking to raise funds for the Institute. This publication implies that the Baptist Institute was created in 1924, although Sasser's history notes an earlier existence. Nevertheless, the Institute was given a new life at Oak Grove and served the community well until 1930. The publication states:

> At a meeting held in the old Oak Grove church-house late in the year 1924, the Jackson County Baptist Institute came into being. Five members, consisting of Jim Brumback, Boyd Farmer, Bige Anderson, and Charlie Farmer, headed by their loyal pastor William Anderson… organized the present school. … [T]he school was formally opened on July 14, 1925.

Perhaps the desks purchased by Armilda Anderson for the Baptist Institute in 1925, were very similar to the desks shown in this picture of a Gray Hawk Community School classroom in 1935. The children in this picture are: front row, left to right, Randall Robinson, Jewell Montgomery, and Jr. Tom Hays; second row, Anna Hunter, Virgie Montgomery, and Dorothy Mullins; third row, Hershel Bennett, Geneva Isaacs, and Vernon Hunter; fourth row, Christine Pierson, Howard Sandlin, and Georgie Pennington; fifth row, Georgie Bennett and Jewell Brumback. (Courtesy of Jewell Montgomery Gabbard)

The enrollment was fifty pupils. Long boards were nailed on the top of the church benches to form desks for the scholars. These desks were a menace to the peace and harmony of both teacher and pupil. … Finally, Aunt Armilda Anderson, the pastor's good wife said "We've got to have some desks; I'll give five dollars for one of them." With a vision of a schoolroom properly furnished, Miss DeLange commenced a canvass of the community which resulted in raising one hundred and fifty dollars with which fifty-five new desks were purchased from Grand Rapids, Michigan. ("A Cry From the Hills of Kentucky," 1928, 2-3)

At the end of the first year, it was apparent that high school grades were needed, and the next school year saw the addition of high school grades and the enrollment of six students. And the following summer, a girls' dormitory was built. Large enough to accommodate twenty girls and the teachers, who previously had boarded in the homes of the community, it was named Oak Grove Dormitory. (Ibid.)

Nevertheless, the school could not be financially sustained; and the Jackson County Baptist Institute, located at what was then known as Wilma, Kentucky, closed after the 1929–30 school year.

The Reformed Church Educational Efforts

In 1900, the Women's Board of Domestic Missions of the Reformed Church in America sent their first missionaries into Jackson County. The women purchased a large cottage in McKee (this eventually became the parsonage of the McKee Reformed Church), and held classes there until the construction in 1904 of the McKee Academy. The academy offered classes for grades one through eight. With the arrival of the Reverend and Mrs. Isaac Messler in 1905, a teacher's cottage was built next to the academy.

In 1907, high school grades were added. This was the first high school in Jackson County. At about the same time, a dormitory was built for girls who lived too far away to walk to school each day.

The McKee Academy, established in 1904 by the Reformed Church in America, was the first high school in Jackson County. To the right of the Academy is the teacher's cottage. (Courtesy of James Earl Hays)

The Reformed Church operated the academy until 1921, when it was leased to the county school system, and became the Jackson County High School. However, the church continued to operate the girls' dormitory for several more years.

Top left: A girls' dormitory was built about 1905 to provide housing for girls who lived too far away to walk each day to school. This building stood where the J. R. Dunsil home stands today. (From the Southern Appalachian Archives of the Berea College Library)

Top right: Shown here is the McKee Academy graduating class of 1913. Pictured left to right are: Dennie Frost, Hugh Collier, Grace Sparks, Stanley Engle, Mary Rosa Turner, and Moss Farmer. (From the Engle Family Collection)

Above: The Gray Hawk Community School, established by the Reformed Church in 1906, moved into the old Hospital building at Gray Hawk about 1927. It later became part of the public school system until further consolidation made it obsolete. It stood across Highway 421 from the Gray Hawk Reformed Church. (Courtesy of JoAnne Moore)

The mission work of the Reformed Church was expanded to Gray Hawk in 1906, and, as with McKee, a school with grades one through eight was established. On Sundays, church services were also held in this building. When the Mary Isabella Allen Hospital was closed in 1927, the two-story hospital building was converted to a single story four-room school, and students moved across the road. The original school building was then built on to and became the church building of the Gray Hawk Reformed Church.

Mission outreach in 1906 also included the building of a log school/church in the Atkins neighborhood on land purchased by a Miss Hoover of Elizabeth, New Jersey.

The Reformed Church began work in Annville in 1909 with the establishment of the Annville Institute, a boarding school for grades one through eight. School opened in 1910 with 37 students; when classes began the next fall, there were 101 students.

Katherine E. Worthington became principal in 1911 and taught a Normal Training Class, which included a review of the eighth grade work, enabling students to qualify for teaching certificates. Total enrollment was 188. In the fall of 1914, 272 students were enrolled. The ninth grade was added the following year and the tenth grade in 1916. Enrollment now stood at 272 students. In 1918, student enrollment reached 365. The eleventh grade became part of the program in 1922. With the addition of grade twelve in the fall of 1923, the school became recognized as a "fully accredited high school;" and, in the spring of 1924, the first high school class of five girls and three boys graduated. (*Annville Institute 1909–1978*, 1998, 9)

Best Friends at their eighth grade graduation from the Gray Hawk Community School in 1937 are left to right: Christine Isaacs, Lecky Brumback, Eunice Sandlin, Anna Hunter, Datha Vickers, Dovie Banks, and Christine Pierson. (Courtesy of JoAnne Moore)

All students were required to work at a job, with jobs changing every six weeks, so that "he may fully appreciate the dignity of labor in making a living." (Ibid., 8)

This program also allowed those who could not pay tuition, to pay expenses through labor.

For almost seventy years, Annville Institute served the people of Jackson County; but declining enrollment and climbing expenses led to its closure in 1978.

The Annville Christian Academy

In 1985, a group of citizens established the Annville Christian Academy. This private

The Annville Institute, a boarding school, was established by the Reformed Church in 1909. Pictured here are Lincoln Hall and Tanis Chapel about 1925. The original Lincoln Hall classroom building was destroyed by fire in 1921. (Courtesy of James Earl Hays)

school started out as pre-school through sixth grade, but now includes seventh and eighth grades. It is located on the campus of Jackson County Ministries, but is owned and operated by parents.

The Annville Christian Academy was established in 1985. Shown here preparing to march in the July 4th parade is the baton team, left to right: Amy York, Felicia Smith, Courtney Marcum, Karen Becknell, Rachel Garland, Jessica Flinchum, and Jenna Allen. Holding the banner are Carolyn York and Richard Garland. (Courtesy of Jessica Flinchum)

LATER YEARS OF CONSOLIDATION

The 1930s saw a move toward the consolidation of many of the one-room (sometimes called one-teacher) schools. This effort was furthered by the New Deal programs of the Roosevelt administration. In Jackson County, educational buildings, public facilities, roads, and bridges were constructed under the supervision of the Works Progress Administration (WPA) and the Civilian Conservation Corps (CCC). As county roads were expanded and improved, and the advent of school buses made longer distances between schools possible, consolidation continued to advance.

The Clover Bottom Elementary School (no longer standing) was typical of consolidated schoolhouses of the 1930s and 40s. Several one-room schools would be consolidated into buildings such as this. (From the Southern Appalachian Archives of the Berea College Library)

In 1936, the WPA built a gymnasium and cafeteria to augment the Tyner School, which, by now, had expanded to house all twelve grades. However, the gymnasium building burned soon after construction. It was then remodeled into classrooms and became the Tyner High School, with a cafeteria located in the basement to serve all grades. The old Tyner School building then housed only grades one through eight.

In 1938, the WPA completed the new McKee High School. Grades five through twelve then moved from the Jackson County High School (the old

McKee Academy) to the brand new McKee High School on the hill overlooking McKee. The lower grades remained at the old McKee Academy building next to the McKee Reformed Church. It is not clear when the old academy building, which had served the county well since 1905, was torn down; but, by the 1950s, school for the lower primary grades was held in a much smaller building, perhaps in the old, lean-to addition to the old building.

In 1938, a new public school was constructed by the WPA on a lot adjacent to the Gray Hawk Reformed Church. The Reformed Church then turned over the Gray Hawk Community School, housed in the old hospital building, to the county for use as a public school. Elementary grades were then divided between the two schools until further consolidation of schools at Tyner and McKee made these buildings obsolete. The old hospital building has been torn down and the present Head Start Program occupies this site. At present, the old WPA school building at Gray Hawk looks much the same, but has been renovated to house a cross-denominational church-based countywide youth program called The Fountain of Youth.

On July 16, 1945, the school year in Jackson County began with a teachers' meeting. Classes began on July 17 for the seventy public schools, many of which were still one-teacher schools. By this time, there were two public high schools (Tyner & McKee) and one private (Annville Institute). Education in grades one through twelve was now accessible to all Jackson County children, and it was state law that they stay in school until they became sixteen years old.

And consolidation continued. Moores Creek School, built in 1946, is an example of the type of consolidation that was taking place across the county. Six one-room schools (Peoples, Bond, Lite, Roy Rader, Greenhill, and Moores Creek) were closed, and students moved into the new Moores Creek School.

The Tyner gymnasium and cafeteria is shown here on the right in about 1936. Constructed by the Works Progress Administration, this building burned not long after this picture was made. It was remodeled into the Tyner High School. The building on the left housed grades one through twelve until the high school grades moved into the renovated gymnasium about 1940. (Courtesy of Jack Norris)

Standing beside the very early school bus for Tyner High School is Roy Moore. Note that the Tyner gymnasium has been destroyed by fire, but not yet remodeled into the high school. (Courtesy of Eldon Bowling)

The Tyner High School is shown here in the 1950s. This building served until the construction of the consolidated Jackson County High School in 1966–67. Flat Rock Furniture Company now occupies this building. (Courtesy of Elaine Madden)

The McKee High School was constructed by the Works Progress Administration in 1938. The building served both primary and secondary grades for many years. (Courtesy of Jack Norris)

Consolidation took a major turn in the early 1950s. Sand Gap Elementary School was built, and several schools were combined to make up the student body of this school. In the late 1950s, Hisel Elementary was built, and five one-room schools were closed. Around the same time, Sand Gap had several more rooms added. Later, a multi-purpose space for a cafeteria and gymnasium was added. The latest addition to Sand Gap occurred in 2005, when the building was renovated and a large library was added.

When McKee Elementary (often called Bill's Branch School) was built in 1965, the early primary grades from the old McKee Academy building were moved there. The older primary students were still housed at the McKee High School. One principal served both buildings, even though they were a couple of miles apart.

The largest move toward consolidation came when the current Jackson County High School opened its doors for the 1966–67 school year. Students were transferred there from Tyner and McKee High Schools. Tyner and McKee were then converted into elementary schools. At this time, all remaining one- and two-room schools were closed. Hisel and Moores Creek were four-room schools and remained open for several more years.

The construction of the Jackson County Middle School in 1990 relieved crowded conditions in all county schools. (Photograph by Fletcher Gabbard)

The three current elementary schools are pictured here. Each of these schools underwent extensive remodeling and renovations in recent years. *Top:* Sand Gap Elementary was built in the early 1950s. *Middle:* McKee Elementary was built about 1965. *Bottom:* Tyner Elementary was built about 1970. (Photographs by Jean Fee)

The Jackson County High School, completed in 1966, combined the McKee and Tyner High Schools into one student body. (Photograph by Fletcher Gabbard)

The Jackson County Area Technology Center, completed in 2001, offers enhanced career opportunities for high school students and adults. Housed within the Technology Center is the Community Theatre, which is available to community groups as well as students. (Photograph by Jean Fee)

In 1985, when an addition to McKee Elementary on Bill's Branch was completed, the upper primary grades moved from the old high school in McKee to the new building. Hisel was closed also, and most of Hisel's students went to McKee; others went to Sand Gap. Moores Creek was closed in 1990, when a new Jackson County Middle School was opened. All sixth, seventh, and eighth grades in the county were transferred to the middle school. The three large elementary schools (McKee, Tyner, and Sand Gap) now housed K-5 grades.

The next big project for Jackson County Public Schools was to build a vocational school. This dream came true on December 1, 2001, when the Jackson County Area Technology Center opened. Students are bused about three miles from the Jackson County High School for classes enhancing and expanding career options that lead to continuation of their education at the post-secondary level and/or successful employment upon graduation from high school.

As late as the 1950s some families still harvested crops without the benefit of machinery. Here Arthur Lakes, with help from family and friends, is shown shocking oats which have been cut with a cradle scythe on the Lakes farm near Wind Cave. (Courtesy of Fletcher Gabbard)

Farming

$\mathcal{A}$griculture has played a significant role in the history of rural America, and that includes Jackson County. Farming is, of course, important because it is our source of food; but becoming a farmer also usually meant becoming a property owner. It was the land—the prospect of owning a piece of property—that enticed the pioneer over the mountains and into the interior. Alexis de Tocqueville recognized this in 1848:

> In no other country in the world is the love of property keener or more alert than in the United States, and nowhere else does the majority display less inclination toward doctrines which in any way threaten the way property is owned.
>
> [From: "Why Great Revolutions Will Become Rare," *Democracy in America (1848)*, Harper & Row edition, 1966, Vol. II, Chap.21, pp.638–639]

EARLY DAYS

The settlers coming through the Cumberland Gap and into Kentucky in the latter part of the 1700s were husbandmen, seeking land to homestead and farm, and bringing with them the basic tools and animals. Harry Toulmin, president of Transylvania Seminary (later University) in Lexington, Kentucky, 1794–96, describes the homesteads of these early settlers:

> In such a situation (after building his house which cost him little more than his labor) he should produce some ... fowls, a cow and a

Pictured here cultivating corn about 1916 are (left to right) John, Frank, Jess, Tilman, and George Seals. The sparse corn population explains why average yields for corn were less than twenty-five bushels per acre during this time period. Today, corn yields are well over one hundred bushels per acre in normal growing seasons. (Courtesy of Lorene Adkins)

breeding sow. The fowls will produce eggs for his family, the cow milk and butter, if she is taken care of; and the sow will produce two, if not three litters of pigs within the year. (Clark. *Agrarian ...*, 1977, 6)

This pattern of subsistence farming sustained the Appalachian farm family for more than a century. Nearly all farm efforts were aimed toward providing food for the family. If there were any surpluses, they were traded for items that the farm couldn't provide. Hunting and trapping were a part of this pattern, providing meat for the table and furs to trade for goods.

Over the years, as more land was cleared, grazing livestock and growing crops began to play greater roles on the family farm, providing more income. The typical early-twentieth century farm in Jackson County consisted of about ninety acres with a garden, chickens, one or two milk cows, a hog that would be fattened and killed for meat, a mule or horse for travel and plowing, a few grazing cattle, and perhaps some sheep. (Hudson, 1996)

Hogs were an important part of the daily food supply in early Jackson County. Most families would kill and process hogs, then salt cure the meat for use throughout the year. Pictured here are Zack Ward, Roy Bingham, Mary Bingham, "One-Armed" Billy Bingham, carrying hot water, and Walter Bingham and George Bingham scraping the hog. (Courtesy of Lorene Adkins)

Chicken and pork were the primary meat sources for the farm family. Chickens provided a ready source of fresh meat and eggs, while pork was easily preserved by salt curing. Beef was eaten rarely since it was much harder to preserve before refrigeration. Most families would slaughter at least one hog a year—and sometimes two. Larger families would often have more livestock to provide for the family. Clyde Boggs, a local farmer and the oldest of fifteen children, said his family would kill six hogs each year, and then salt and cure the meat for the winter ahead.

Eliza and General Bowling stand among their flock of chickens. Chickens were among the most important farm animal in the early years of Jackson County, not only because of their immediate availability as meat and eggs for the table, but also because of their value in trading for other staples, such as sugar, salt, or flour. (Courtesy of Glenna Carpenter)

Wallace Lakes, who grew up in the Horse Lick area of Jackson County and has been significantly involved in agriculture all his life, recalled, in an interview, the importance of chickens and the garden plot on the family farm:

> …chickens may have been the most important farm animals during the early years of Jackson County because of their immediate availability to the breakfast and dinner tables for farm families. And the eggs could be traded for other goods the family would need, such as sugar, flour, salt, and baking powder. Farmers also raised chickens for markets, taking them to local stores where they were purchased for resale to larger markets.

> The garden was the most important parcel of land on the farm since this is where the majority of the food the family would consume throughout the year came from. The produce was used fresh or it would be preserved through canning, drying, or pickling. A cellar would provide storage for potatoes as well as the canned goods.

Lakes talked of how everyone in the family would contribute to the efforts for the upkeep and maintenance of the farm, from the oldest member to the youngest member of the family. Everyone in the household had chores that they were responsible for on a daily and sometimes seasonal basis.

While most farms had at least one or two milk cows, some would have seven to ten

The family garden was crucial to early farm families and was typically located on the best parcel of land near the house. Pictured here are I. J. Lake and Nan Parrett preparing a garden spot in the Seven Pines area of Jackson County in 1945. (Courtesy of Dena Lakes Burgess)

These ladies are preparing a chicken for Sunday dinner—a favorite time for gathering together family and friends. Here, in the 1940s, Nan Parrett, standing in the center, oversees the scalding of the chicken by the younger generation: Irene Vaughn on the left and Bessie Parrett (later Lakes) on the right. (Courtesy of Dena Lakes Burgess)

cows that were milked by hand, and surplus milk would be sold. The milk was kept cool in natural springs on or near the farm or dropped by rope into the well. Clyde Boggs said that most of the milk consumed by his family was in the form of buttermilk. Families would churn their own butter as well. Since the family usually only needed one or two dairy cows, the calves would either be sold as veal or kept to replace an existing cow.

Wallace Lakes recounts a time when there were cream stations in the county. There were several locations throughout the county but the largest one may have been in the Bond community. At these stations, the cream would be tested for butter fat content, and cream companies would come once a week and purchase cream from the farmers, basing the price upon the butter fat content. The cream would be taken to East Bernstadt on Monday where it was loaded on a train and sent to Cincinnati. According to Clyde Boggs, "large crowds of people gathered at the cream station at Bond on Saturdays to sell cream, but it was far from a social gathering. They waited in line to sell their cream to get money to buy supplies and get back to the farm to continue their chores."

Most cattle and some hogs that were raised were sold to local buyers who would drive them to Richmond to market. Boggs recalls, "It took two days to drive cattle or hogs to Richmond to the market from Tyner and one day on a horse or mule to get back home. There were boarding houses along the way that would pen up the livestock and provide a place for the farmers to sleep before going on the next day to market." Most of the cattle and hogs raised during this time were crossbred. It was not until the 1950s that pure bred livestock were introduced into the county.

George Samuel Roach watches his cow and new calf in a 1940s farm scene near Annville. Milk cows were important to the family in providing milk for the table, and families with several cows would sell surplus milk and the cream as an added income source to the farm. (Courtesy of George Roach)

Some families raised sheep—largely for the extra income from the sale of wool and lambs, but also for food. They would shear the sheep in May and either sell the wool or send it to woolen mills to be made into yarn or other goods in exchange for a portion of the wool. In the 1983 spring issue of *Kentucky Heritage*, a magazine of the Kentucky Junior Historical Society, there is an account of Wesley Morgan's grandfather, John Wesley Davis, who was a wool agent for the Riverside Woolen Mills in Knoxville, Tennessee, in the late 1800s. He visited the various farms, collecting the wool to be sent to the mill to be made into linsey and flannel. Mr. Davis would then take the woolen products, which had been requested, back to the people. In some cases, people requested yarn which would then be used to make socks, gloves, or "toboggans" (knitted hats). The lambs would be sold around September. One of the most important aspects of raising sheep was the provision of extra income at a time in the year before crops were harvested.

Horses and mules played a role in the early farms of Jackson County. In fact, farm production data show that in the first fifty years of the county the number of horses and mules increased over four hundred percent (Kentucky Agricultural Statistical Service). This increase coincided with an increased acreage in crops. Although the farm would need to increase production in order to feed the additional animals, the animals made it easier to plant and harvest, leading to increased production.

The major crops grown on these early farms were corn and tobacco. The corn was grown on rough land. Statistics from the time indicate that corn was important, but yields were small, suggesting that the corn was grown primarily as a food source for the livestock. In 1910, an average of twelve bushels of corn were produced per acre; whereas, in 2007, corn production averaged well over one hundred bushels per acre.

Even though tobacco had been grown since the earliest settlers arrived in Jackson County, the commercial growth of tobacco didn't take off until the 1910s or 20s. The U. S. Census shows that 18,983 pounds of tobacco were produced in 1910, but in 1930 there were 906,334 pounds produced. Tobacco prices early on were minimal but slowly increased, until tobacco became a significant cash crop for Jackson County farms. Clyde Boggs recalls, "It took a day with a wagon and team to get to the top of Big Hill with a load of tobacco. They would make it to Richmond by midday on the second day with their tobacco crop."

John Wesley Davis was a wool merchant, collecting wool from local farmers and sending it off to woolen mills, where woolen products were made. The farmers received a portion of the products in exchange for the wool. Mr. Davis is pictured here with his family in the early 1900s. In the back row, left to right are Willy, Minerva, Lizzie, Ellen and Charley. Seated are John, John Wesley, and Telitha Cook Davis. (Courtesy of Ruth Morgan Combs)

Not all wool was sent to the woolen mills. Some was retained to spin into yarn for knitting during the winter months. Jane Roach Powell is seen here spinning wool into yarn in the early 1900s. (Courtesy of George Roach)

The old flour mill at Peoples (still standing today) was operated by Allen Davidson from the 1920s until his death in 1943. His son-in-law, Ed Denham, then took over. After World War II, production tapered off, and the mill closed in the mid-1950s. (Courtesy of Roma Baker)

DID YOU KNOW...

■ ■ ■

that blackberries were once an important cash crop in the county—or that hemp was grown during World War II? Blackberries were found everywhere and cost nothing except the time to pick them. In 1928, buyers were paying a nickel per gallon, and by the 1940s, the price had risen to ten cents per gallon. In 1931, *The Jackson County Sun* reported that the principal occupation in Egypt in July of that year was picking blackberries. And the demand for hemp during World War II led to its brief re-establishment as a legitimate crop.

Boggs remembers being at the tobacco warehouse when prices reached one dollar per pound and hearing a thunderous roar of excitement from the farmers throughout the warehouse.

Boggs further recalled that tobacco barns started being constructed in the 1930s. "Barn construction was a community effort. The men of the community would come together and build the barn while the women would cook a meal. All of this occurred before there was any government support for tobacco growers," said Boggs.

TRANSITIONS

The first Agricultural Extension Agent in the county, Walker Reynolds, was appointed in 1914, marking the beginning of the move in Jackson County from subsistence farming to more emphasis on farm income. There was a steady increase in production during the 1920s; but significant gains in crop yields began to occur in the 1930s, when lime and fertilizer practices were emphasized.

Livestock numbers also began to increase during the 1930s and 40s. And the introduction of pure bred livestock in 1950 coincides with a noticeable increase in the number of cattle and hogs raised in the county.

Grinding sorghum cane with a mule, in preparation for making molasses, was once commonplace. Today, this process has been mechanized. (Courtesy of Jess Wilson)

World War II had a profound effect on the agricultural environment in Jackson County. The labor force was reduced significantly because many able young men left for the war effort. And, after the war, many left for the factories of the North. There was an effort by the government to encourage the return to the farms. Lakes recalls that "after the war, agriculture in the county accelerated because of veterans on farm training programs. Veterans were paid to go to agriculture schools." This consisted of two hours of class a week and farming. Wallace Lakes taught at such a school, and Clyde Boggs attended one for two years.

Mechanization and the advent of electricity helped offset some of the labor lost to the industrial North. Dairies soon began milking cows with machines and cooling the milk in bulk milk tank refrigeration systems. Tractors began to replace mules and horses in the late 1940s, and mechanized equipment, such as hay balers, followed in the early 1950s. Clyde Boggs and his father-in-law, Everett Jones, were partners in buying a tractor in January of 1950. For about a two thousand dollar investment, they were able to buy a tractor, a two-way plow, a mowing machine, and a harrow. Today, this equipment would be tens of thousands of dollars for only the minimum equipment needed on the farm.

Although mechanization and the advent of electricity helped offset the loss of labor for a time, the problem resurfaced in the early 1990s, and farm labor shortages continue.

Kim Solomon, left and Chris Hornsby, right, help their grandfather, G. Buck Hornsby, in the 1980s, cook off the sorghum syrup produced by grinding the cane. The resulting sorghum molasses would then be poured into jars for enjoyment in the winter months—or in earlier days might have been sold to produce added income for the farmstead. (Courtesy of Bobby Hornsby)

Tobacco became increasingly important over the years. And the stabilization of tobacco production and markets, through a federal quota system put in place in 1938, made this the most important crop grown on the farm—providing a stable and reliable income. This allowed many producers to buy and pay for their farms through the years. Lending institutions would make loans with payment schedules based on when the tobacco crop would be sold. Farms with large tobacco quotas had a higher per acre land value as well.

Tobacco grown in Jackson County reached a peak production of 4,395,000 pounds in 1982. Production then leveled off around the 3,000,000 pound level. In the early

Pictured here setting tobacco in 1955 are Moss Gabbard, driving, Cap Jones and Ova Gene Gabbard riding the setter, and Jim Jones following. Today, even with more modern equipment and a newer generation of people, this scene is very much the same across Jackson County's landscape at tobacco setting time. (Courtesy of Fletcher Gabbard)

THE TOBACCO QUOTA SYSTEM

■ ■ ■

To reduce the risk to tobacco growers of cyclical and seasonal price changes because of weather and production issues, the federal government began operating programs to support and stabilize tobacco prices in the early 1930s. The Agriculture Adjustment Act of 1933 designated tobacco as a storable commodity, and cash payments were made to producers who restricted production. The Agricultural Act of 1938 authorized marketing quotas, with a penalty for growers who exceeded them, and price supports up to seventy-five percent of parity began. There were many legislative changes after 1938, but they all were made to maintain an adequate and balanced flow of tobacco through the tobacco quota marketing system. In 1941, the Burley Tobacco Growers Cooperative Association or the "pool" began operation, and new allotments were formed to control production. The pool would take tobacco on the market that companies refused to purchase because of quality, tobacco type, excess production, etc. and pay the producers the support price for the tobacco. They would then take the tobacco, process it, and sell to the companies in years when supply was short or certain grades or stalk positions were in higher demand. The tobacco program was not a subsidy; it was a loan program. The quota system provided an acreage allotment for each producer, and formulas based on world supply and demand for tobacco were used to set prices each year. Having a tobacco quota assigned to a farm added value to the land. In 1971, a new program of control was put into effect to both limit acreage and poundage. In 1975, the acreage part of the program was dropped. Throughout the 1980s and 1990s, several legislative acts were passed to control and adjust prices and/or quota to meet worldwide demand and company needs. Sometimes there would be an increase and other times a decrease in poundage, prices, or both. In 1999, a substantial cut to quota occurred, followed by another forty-five percent reduction in 2000. Talks of a buyout of the tobacco quota began to increase, and, in 2004, the tobacco program, as it had been known for decades, ended. Beginning with the 2005 production year, tobacco producers began to contract their crop and market directly to tobacco companies. (Information provided by Dr. Gary Palmer, University of Kentucky Tobacco Specialist, 2007)

1900s, Kentucky's Long-Term Policy Research Center identified Jackson County as one of the fifteen most tobacco-dependent counties in the state. By 1998, over sixty percent of the total farm cash receipts of $12 million was from tobacco. In 2004, receipts were $7,600,000, (only about half from tobacco), and production had fallen to about 1,600,000 pounds, reflecting the reduction in quotas, which had begun in the late 1990s.

In 2004, the national tobacco quota program ended. After years of controversy surrounding tobacco production and discussions between the tobacco companies, the government, and the tobacco industry leadership, the national tobacco quota was bought out.

Tobacco was more than a farm enterprise to Jackson County; it was a way of life—and is still today, only to a much less extent. By 2007, tobacco production in the county was down to six hundred thousand pounds, about the amount grown in the 1920s. Offsetting this reduction is the buyout provision of $17 million to Jackson County farmers over a ten-year period. This $1.7 million contribution, added to a crop value of about $1 million in 2007, cannot come close to providing the past contributions of tobacco to the Jackson County farmer and economy. With the decline of tobacco, farmers in the county have turned to beef cattle production and diversified crop production.

Agriculture in Jackson County has evolved from subsistence farming, with many small farms (about 2,500 in 1939) to more commercial farming with larger, but fewer farms (only 727 in 2004). Although there are fewer farms, crops and products are being grown on a larger scale on fewer acres. Today, farmers not only provide for their own family, but also help to provide food for the rest of the world. Today, meat and produce are commercially grown, and most families depend upon someone else to provide food for their families in this fast-paced society.

Standing among tobacco curing structures on their farm are three generations of tobacco farmers: Clyde Boggs, in the center, with his grandson Chris on the left and son Ricky on the right. Mr. Boggs grew the first tobacco crop of his own in 1946, after helping his family grow theirs as a boy. These three grew their last crop in 2004. (Courtesy of the Jackson County Extension Service)

No longer does every family grow a garden—in fact, very few do. Most gardens grown in Jackson county today are grown by the older generation—a generation that can remember an earlier time when gardens were necessary. These folk still have a real appreciation for growing and preserving a large percentage of their food. Presently, in the early twenty-first century, Jackson County is far from a fast-paced society, but when it comes to food production and consumption, the county mirrors the rest of society.

Over the centuries, agriculture has cultivated a dependable work force, close-knit communities, and strong family units. These qualities, that were so prevalent in the early years when farm life impacted nearly everyone in the county, are still evident in the close-knit, agricultural community of Jackson County today.

Mary Moore's family entitled this picture: "the last tobacco crop before the buyout;" a poignant reminder of the changing nature of farming in the twenty-first century. (Courtesy of Mary Moore)

This picture of the Bond-Foley Lumber Company in the 1920s shows the company commissary, in the center, and next to it on the right is the company office (later the Bond Sewing Factory) and next to that (only partially shown) is the Bond State Bank. These buildings faced the old road, with train tracks behind them. Note the train engine behind the bank. These tracks later became Highway 30, and the old road was abandoned. (Courtesy of Jack Norris)

Business & *Industry*

The first businesses in the county were most likely the general stores—every little community had one. As the population grew and roads improved, business and services expanded. Chapter 3 described businesses (largely retail) within communities. This chapter will describe the extractive industries of lumber and coal, the growth of the banking industry, and the latter-day establishment of the manufacturing industry.

Lumber

From an early date, settlers cut timber—first to clear land, build homes, and burn for heat. Later, logging on a small scale provided a cash crop to buy necessities. It was not until the 1870s that large logging operations of the East, which had exhausted the eastern timber stands of New England and the lake states, began to look toward the forests of the West and South. The southern uplands, where the slow progress of mechanization had to some extent spared the lush forests, were a rich prize. Jackson County, Kentucky, with its wide-spread stands of virgin timber, was highly attractive to those seeking their fortunes in the lumber business. The Turkeyfoot Lumber Company and the Bond-Foley Lumber Company were the major timber companies operating in the county in the early decades of the 1900s.

BOND-FOLEY LUMBER COMPANY

The glory that was Bond has all but disappeared. The raucous and strident mill, hurling out millions of board feet of finished lumber, is now no more than some large concrete pylons sticking out of the ground. The state bank, horse stables, company store, apartment houses, theater, community center, train station, and other such manifestations of an industrial town have given way to a few residences and a small strip mall.

In partnership with Mr. Foley, of the Foley Furniture Factory in Herkimer, New York, Mr. Ninian Ulysses Bond came to the small farming community of Isaacs, Kentucky, in 1913, seeking to buy and process the fine hardwoods that were a major feature of the local landscape. Isaacs, Kentucky, later re-named Bond in honor of the mill founder, was a community of subsistence farmers and a few general stores. The land, not much suited to commercial

Ninian Ulysses Bond, in conjunction with Mr. Foley of the Foley Furniture Factory in Herkimer, New York, founded the Bond-Foley Lumber Company in the little town of Isaac, Kentucky, in 1913. He later became a Kentucky state senator. The name of the town was changed to Bond in his honor. (Courtesy of Glennwood McQueen)

James Pingleton, timekeeper for the mill operation, is shown here with his clock and lunch bucket. He is about sixty-three years old, and that may explain why he has a less strenuous job. Most likely, he kept the time of the workers at the mill, and he may have timed the various sawmilling tasks. He was killed in 1922 by a board thrown from a saw. Mr. Pingleton is buried at the York Cemetery in Bond/Annville. (Courtesy of Darryl Pingleton)

farming, was acceptable for grazing; consequently, cattle, hogs, sheep, and poultry were in abundance. Several locals added to their income by buying and driving livestock to markets in London and Richmond. The coming of Mr. N. U. Bond was to precipitate major changes in this localized economy.

Approximately twenty-five thousand acres of timber and the mineral rights that went with the land were originally purchased by Mr. Bond and his agents. These land holdings, both leased and purchased, were to expand to some forty thousand acres or more during the sixteen years that the mill was in full operation. By several estimates, around two hundred men were employed by the Bond-Foley Mill. Most were deployed to work in the forest areas while a little more than a quarter of the worker population remained at the mill works in Bond. (Hudson, 1996)

The mill itself was one of the largest in the United States. It was a double-band mill with one blade cutting quarter-sawn wood almost continuously. Wood sawed in this fashion displayed the grain more dramatically, thus making it suited to the manufacture of fine furniture. The secondary blade cut wood for other, less-refined purposes. The mill had the capacity to produce twenty million board feet of finished lumber per year. (Bowles [1919]) The fact that the mill ran nearly continuously for almost sixteen years is a testament to the enormous number of white oak, pine, poplar, chestnut, black oak, and hickory trees that once graced these hills.

With an operation of this magnitude came many corollary businesses. One of the most impressive and useful was the Rockcastle River Railway. Since local roads were poor or non-existent, an efficient method for getting wood products to the train station near London was absolutely necessary. Mr. Bond applied for and was granted permission to build a railway

Men, machines, and mules combine forces to create one of the largest industrial endeavors ever to take place in Jackson County. A typical logging scene shows mules pulling logs into the loading area where they are being loaded on rail cars. Walter C. Schrencegost operated this loading car. (Courtesy of Glennwood McQueen)

from East Bernstadt to the Bond mill. This track was later extended to points in McKee. The train was a boon, not only to businesses, but also to passengers.

Regularly scheduled excursions carried a significant passenger load from Bond to East Bernstadt. The track stayed in regular usage until most mill operations ceased in 1930. The land owned by the railway company was donated to the state of Kentucky for highway purposes, with Highway 30 now where the track once lay.

The company commissary, later known as Tom Coffey's store, was another corollary business of the lumber company. It accepted both cash and company scrip for supplies of all kinds. Everything from seeds to saw blades to coffin-making supplies could be bought.

Also springing up around the mill were numerous other business concerns. A doctor's office and the Bond State Bank brought needed services, not only to mill workers, but to all people of the immediate area. Restaurants and a liquor store helped supply more temporal needs to those who were interested. Even movies were shown in the community building that was later moved from Bond Hill to become the meeting place for Bond Baptist Church.

All things come to a close, and the Bond-Foley Mill was no exception. The supply of trees dwindled, and the operations began to decline until tree cutting stopped in March 1930. The mill was abandoned the following May. The last of the available lumber was sold by early 1932, and the railway closed the same year.

The legacy Bond-Foley left behind was a mixed one. Mr. Bond made some enemies, as can be seen in his correspondence with business associates and lawsuits with locals. These people characterized him as a "hornswoggler," but others remember him as a hero and friend. Former employees have recalled their Bond-Foley days by testifying that they were treated fairly and that the company was a source of pride for Jackson County. Employees were paid good wages, and company scrip could be spent at stores other than the company's. Company housing was available, but many employees chose to remain at home and commute, retaining their ties to family farms. Several locals rose to positions of leadership in the company. Kentuckians even elected Mr. Bond as a senator. Furthermore, Mr. Bond (although not a native of the county) established family ties here when he married Annville's postmistress. Although he moved away when the company closed, his family continued to visit the county for years.

The story of Bond-Foley does not fit perfectly with that of the typical company town of the period. The popular image of coal and timber towns in Appalachia is one of stark exploitation. According to this narrative, outside investors came to the region, swindled hard-pressed farmers out of their land, and exploited their cheap labor. When they parted with their homesteads, they also lost their independence and found themselves living in company towns that ensnared them in an endless cycle of debt.

Important work has been done on the history of timber towns in Appalachia; however, a comprehensive study of Bond-Foley remains to be done. Not only is the story of Bond-Foley of great historical significance to Jackson County, it is also a crucial part of the larger story of Appalachian industrialization. A wealth of information awaits some scholar who will piece together

Bond-Foley furnished its workers with these portable "apartments." These dwellings could be placed on flatcars and taken to work sites throughout the area. This is the camp at Bond in 1925. (From the Fred De Jong Collection, courtesy of the De Jong family)

the puzzle. There are scattered interviews, articles, and private collections of photographs at the Jackson County Public Library. This substantial collection includes land deeds, maps, ledger books, and correspondence.

The history of Bond-Foley is far too rich to be captured in a few pages, but hopefully these will inspire someone to write a full-length history of the subject someday. Perhaps such a person will address some of the questions raised here. Why was Mr. Bond considered a "hornswaggler" by some, but not by others? Were the company's land holdings acquired honestly, dishonestly, or both? Did some of it change hands because of hard times and non-payment of taxes? Who were the people who sued him, and did many of them leave the area after losing their land? How did he intend to dispose of the land after the timber was removed? Could he have sold it to locals, or was the government's offer his only option?

If such a study is conducted fairly, it will likely conclude that Mr. Bond was something between a villain and a hero—a human being whose short-lived company left an enduring (although mixed) legacy to the people of Jackson County. Millions of dollars were made, and the terrain of the county was changed forever. Only a very few are now living who can remember the mill, but it is and will remain an indelible component of local history.

THE TURKEYFOOT LUMBER COMPANY

Turkeyfoot Lumber Company, based in Huntington, West Virginia, operated in Jackson County at about the same time as Bond-Foley and mostly cut in the northeastern part of the county. Its mill was located at Cressmont in Lee County.

Joe Sparks, interviewed in 2007, recalled the days when Turkeyfoot provided employment. Joe's Father, Bill Sparks, born in 1904, went to work for the Turkeyfoot Lumber Company when he was fifteen years old. Joe remembers his father's stories:

> Dad talked about the large steam skidders which were used to pull up logs from the valley floors to the ridges where the trains could haul them to the mill. There were railroads running out 89 North and to Wind Cave and to Sand Lick, and lots of other places—right along the ridges. You can still find the railroad beds on the ridges around Wind Cave.
>
> Dad also worked for the Bond-Foley Company after the Turkeyfoot Company had logged out. He said that one day, he and his partner, using a two man saw, came up on a section of trees so large that they couldn't cut through them—their saw was not long enough. So new saws were ordered, two feet longer than the ones they were using, and they were able to cut them down. Dad said, "You could saw all day and not see your partner."

Darvel Barrett also recalled stories of the Turkeyfoot Lumber Company: "My father, Tom Barrett, began working there as a young man—probably in the 1890s—drove a team of mules snaking out logs; they cut in the winter and sawed up the logs in the spring when the sap was down. But they didn't cut everything—just the very best to use for furniture."

A skidder, sometimes called "the donkey," was used to pull logs from a valley floor or out of the woods to be piled near the rail tracks for future loading. The men in this picture are unidentified. (Courtesy of Glennwood McQueen)

THE DANIEL BOONE NATIONAL FOREST

The Daniel Boone National Forest (originally named the Cumberland National Forest) contains about seven hundred thousand acres in twenty-one counties of eastern Kentucky. It was created as a direct result of the extensive logging done in the mountains of eastern Kentucky in the first decades of the twentieth century. Recognizing the devastating effect of deforested watersheds, the Weeks Act of 1911 authorized the federal government to purchase lands for stream-flow protection and to maintain the lands as national forests.

In 1933, the government began buying lands for the Cumberland National Forest. The principal land holdings which formed the basis for the new forest were the Stearns Coal and Lumber Company tract of 48,000 acres in McCreary County, the Castle-Craig Coal Company tract of 27,000 acres in Laurel County, and the Warfork Land Company tract of 21,600 acres in Jackson County. (Collins, 1975, 210) Also purchased about the same time were 21,500 acres from the Bond-Foley Lumber Company. (U.S. Forest Service)

The establishment of the CCC camps, which were expanding rapidly in eastern Kentucky in 1933, enabled the forest service to immediately begin improvements on the lands that were being purchased, beginning in 1933. Roads, lookout towers, telephone lines, and campgrounds were constructed by the young men of the CCC. (Collins, 1975, 217) In 1937, the Cumberland National Forest was officially established.

It was not long before timber management was added to the mission of stream protection, and, for years, the forests were managed to provide timber for the nation. In more recent times, timber cutting has all but disappeared; and today, in 2007, the forests are managed for multiple uses, including recreation and wildlife diversity.

With the closure of Bond-Foley and Turkeyfoot Lumber companies, came the establishment of the Daniel Boone National Forest. In the 1930s, the CCC (Civilian Conservation Corps) built fire towers, telephone lines, and campgrounds. Pictured here are some of the "CCC boys" posing at the completed Drip Rock Fire Tower. (Courtesy of Regina Brewer)

In Jackson County, the national forest covers over fifty-nine thousand acres (about twenty-five percent of the land). There are two national recreational areas located in the county: Turkeyfoot and S-Tree. In addition, the Sheltowee Trace, a national recreational hiking trail runs through the county.

Small sawmills have always been a part of Jackson County's economy—both before the coming and after the leaving of the large lumber. These entrepreneurs have rigged a portable sawmill in 1934. From left to right are Fee Baker, Homer Davidson, and Leonard Baker. (Courtesy of Roma Baker)

With its mill located outside the county, Turkeyfoot never became the bustling enterprise that was Bond-Foley. No town grew up, and except for a commissary located where the Turkeyfoot Campground is now, and a boarding house on Hurd Springs Road, there was little commercial activity.

From 1935 to 1939, the Warfork Land Company (the land-holding portion of the Turkeyfoot Lumber Company) sold a total of 21,600 acres to the U.S. Government as a part of the original purchase unit for the Daniel Boone National Forest. The Bond-Foley Lumber Company sold about the same acreage to the government.

COAL

People have always mined coal in Jackson County. Farmers could often find a coal bank on their property to supply coal for the winter. But commercial coal mining did not begin until 1931, with the opening of a mine by the Harrison Coal Company in Harrison Hollow. This mine employed eleven men and produced three thousand tons of coal its first year of operation. By 1936, about fifty-seven companies were operating in the county, producing almost 150,000 tons that year. Annual production leveled off at an average of about 200,000 tons until the outbreak of World War II, when production soared to a peak production of 329,000 tons in 1942. (Kentucky Department of Mines and Minerals)

During the 1930s, coal was an important industry in Jackson County. One of the largest operations was the Scrivner-Moore Coal Company with operations in Moore Hollow near Sand Gap. Here trucks are lined up to be loaded with coal. The large two-story structure in the center of this picture is a hotel, and in the upper right-hand corner is pictured a miner's camp home. (Courtesy of Susan Adams Isaacs and Leroy Adams)

In these early years of coal mining, Moore Hollow was probably the richest coal producing area in the county. The first mine in the hollow was opened in 1933 by Fred and Charlie Pennington (Sand Gap Coal Company). Within a year, they leased it to the Wilkerson brothers from East Bernstadt and then to C. E. Rogers. Also opening mines in the hollow were the Scrivner-Moore Company and Bill Dean, both leasing from the landowner, N. U. Bond. Eventually, the Jackson County Coal Company, owned by M. K. Marlowe, bought out Scrivner-Moore.

The Moore Hollow became almost a town in itself. There was a modern motel built by N. U. Bond in 1939, and run by Caroline Isaacs; a pool hall and restaurant; a commissary; and houses for the workers. As the demand for coal declined during the final years of World War II and immediately after, the mines began to close.

But production surged again in 1950 to over 650,000 tons. This was the first year of significant production from surface mining (70,000 tons). Until 1947, all mining in the county was underground. Production decreased in 1951, and the decline continued until the OPEC (Organization of the Petroleum Exporting Countries) oil embargo of 1973 created a strong demand for coal. In 1976, Jackson County produced a record 807,000 tons, seventy-five percent from surface mining. Production dropped to about 250,000 tons the next year and has fluctuated from year to year since then: back up to 418,000 tons in 1984, to zero in 1996, and 53,000 tons in 2004. Since 1984, almost all production has been from surface mines. (Kentucky Department of Mines and Minerals)

Although coal mining brought economic benefits to the county and its people, it also took its toll. Underground mining was hazardous work. Fletcher Gabbard remembers that his uncle, Sherman Cook, quit working in the mines and moved to Ohio to work in the factories after a roof cave-in killed a fellow worker. A similar story is told by Odis Isaacs, who left the mines after the tragic death of Howard Smith. (*The Jackson County Sun*, 1986)

Howard Wayne Smith Jr., was a very young child when his father was killed in January of 1946. He does not remember his father, but relates the family story:

> The family was a coal-mining family, following the mines from Tennessee to Alabama, and finally to Kentucky, where Jessee Smith, my grandfather, found work in the Blue Diamond Mines in Perry County. In the late 1930s, the family moved to Sand Gap to work the mines. My father, Howard, married Ruby Standafer in 1942 before joining the Air Force. He was discharged in November of 1945, and just two months later was killed in the mines.

Howard Sr. is buried in the Tal Martin Cemetery at Sand Gap.

Another tragedy took the lives of six men, including a fourteen-year-old boy, James Hensley, when a powder cache

Coal mines are dangerous places, and underground mining is particularly so. Howard Smith, who hailed from a coal-mining family, returned from service in World War II only to lose his life in a mine accident in 1946. Staff Sergeant Smith is pictured here on duty. (Courtesy of Howard Smith Jr.)

exploded. The local story is that an argument resulted in a gun being fired into the powder house at the mine station near Sand Gap, where men gathered to get their checks. Also killed in the blast were Elmer and Leonard Clemons, brothers, Tom Johnson, Charlie Harrison, and Bill Beatty. (Sparks, 1983)

BANKING

The early 1900s saw the establishment of two chartered banks in Jackson County: the Jackson County Bank in 1904 and the Bond State Bank in 1917. The Jackson County Bank continues to provide banking services to the citizens of Jackson County. The Bond State Bank, however, provided services only until 1930, closing when the Bond-Foley Lumber Mill closed.

In 1995, Citizen's Bank opened its doors in Jackson County. Following is a closer look at these two thriving institutions.

Jackson County Bank

The Jackson County Bank began as a branch of the Berea Bank and Trust in 1904. In 1909, it was chartered as the Jackson County Bank with assets of fifteen thousand dollars. It is now the oldest business in the county, providing banking services for over one hundred years.

James Randall Hays (known as "JR" or "Jimmy") was the bank's cashier for the first fifty years of its history. In the early days, the duties of a branch

James R. Hays stands here in front of the newly constructed Jackson County Bank in the 1930s. This building, which was the second building to house the bank, has since been added onto, but still retains the original front door and lobby of the bank. (Courtesy of Bruce Hays)

banker were a truly hands-on, do-everything affair. From 1904–1909, in addition to serving customers every day, Mr. Hays also took the deposits of the bank to Berea, riding horseback over Big Hill every Friday afternoon and back on Saturday morning. This was, of course, only during those five years that the bank was part of the larger Berea bank. But his sister, Lou Hays Fowler, whose home was where the bank parking lot is now, also carried extra duties. Each evening, at home, she would write up all the deposits and withdrawals in preparation for banking the next morning.

In 1933, when President Roosevelt declared the Bank Holiday and ordered all banks to close their doors to keep people from making runs on the banks, Mr. Hays stood at the door of the Jackson County Bank with a handful of cash and asked if anyone wanted to take out their money. Only one person did, and they later offered to redeposit it.

Pictured inside the Jackson County Bank are J. R. Hays, cashier from 1904–1954, Russell Hays, president of the bank from 1954–76, and Jim H. Hays Sr. (Courtesy of Nell Hays Westbrook)

Following Mr. J. R. Hays' tenure as head of the bank was his son, Russell, who served as president from 1954 until 1976. Upon the retirement of Russell in 1976, his cousin, James H. Hays Jr., assumed the presidency and, in 2007, still serves in that capacity.

Bruce Hays, the youngest son of J. R. Hays, was affiliated with the bank for over fifty-five years, serving as vice-president and director. Other longtime employees of the bank include Joyce Dunsil, who started work there in 1959, and Woodrow Masters, who began in 1962.

The success of the bank has allowed for the opening of two branch banks, one in Annville in 1977 and one in Sand Gap in 1979. In 1983, the McKee office began acquiring adjoining properties for an extensive expansion. The project, which more than doubled the space, was completed in 1990.

Current CEO, Kendall Norris, who assumed that position upon the death of June Welch in 2006, noted, "It is the people of Jackson County who have made the Jackson County Bank the success that it is today."

James H. Hays Jr. assumed presidency of the Jackson County Bank in 1976 and serves still in that capacity in 2007. (Courtesy of the Jackson County Bank)

Jackson County Bank has grown from a small brick building to this impressive structure which stands at the corner of Main and First Street in McKee. (Courtesy of the Jackson County Bank)

Citizens Bank

Citizens Bank opened its doors in McKee on October 10, 1995, as a branch of Citizens Bank of Brodhead in Rockcastle County. The parent bank was organized in December 1904, by a group of prominent citizens from the community of Brodhead. The following January the bank was launched, with J. Thomas Cherry as president. The bank moved from the old building it had occupied for fifty-eight years to a new facility in 1962. And, in 1985, this space was renovated.

The bank's success over the years made it advisable to open a branch office in Mount Vernon in 1988; this office now serves as Citizens Bank's main office. The branch office in McKee was opened in 1995, as has been noted, and, in 2006, a branch in Somerset was opened.

The current president is Corey C. Craig, who took office in July 2004. Cheryl Rose, branch manager and loan officer at McKee stated in an interview: "Citizens Bank has been an asset to the community of Jackson County. There was no competition before the bank came into the community, and the people of our county now have a choice. Their needs are our ultimate goal, and all of us at Citizens Bank are proud to be a part of Jackson County."

Citizens Bank was established in McKee in 1995, occupying this handsome structure at the corner of U.S. 421 and Education Drive. (Photograph by Jean Fee)

MANUFACTURING

Small-scale manufacturing enterprises have long been a source of pride in Jackson County. The pioneer years of self-reliance led necessarily to a multitude of talents, such as chair-caning, wood-working, iron-working, weaving, and sewing. There was always someone in the community who could perform these tasks and to whom others turned for supply.

It is not surprising that the industrial growth of the 1960s capitalized on these talents. In 1968, Job Start Corporation, now known as Kentucky Highlands Investment Corporation, began a sewing operation called Mountain Toy Makers (later, Possum Trot Toys)— producing unique stuffed animals, which sold nationally. The sewing factory began operations in the community building of the McKee Reformed Church before moving into the first building in the McKee Industrial Park. Much of the credit for the creative designs of the stuffed toys and success of the company goes to Nora Van Winkle.

After the toy manufacturing industry shifted overseas, Laura Ashley, the famed British design company of women's and children's clothing, operated out of the McKee Industrial Park. In 1990, the building was sold to McKee Manufacturing, still a sewing factory; and, in 1995, Specialty Plastics began operations. The McKee Industrial Park now houses BAE Systems, which manufactures defense products and employs several hundred people.

Other early industries were the Christmas Wreath Factory (1968–1999), started by the Christian Appalachian Project (CAP); Kentucky Woodcrafts,

Top left: Among the earliest manufacturers in Jackson County was Possum Trot, which made unique stuffed toys. Pictured here in the 1960s is Nora Van Winkle, standing, and Anita Hayes. (Courtesy of Jess Wilson)

Top right: Visiting the Armor Holdings plant (now BAE Systems) in McKee about 2004, are left to right: State Representative Marie Rader, State Senator Albert Robinson, Mike Hayes of Kentucky Highlands Investment Corporation, and U. S. Congressman Hal Rogers. Others are unidentified. (Courtesy of Jackson County EZ Community, Inc.)

Above: Phoenix Products and Phoenix Poke Boats are once again housed in Jackson County at the Northern Jackson County Industrial Park. (Photograph by Jean Fee)

started by CAP in 1967, but operated by Kentucky Highlands Investment Corporation from 1980 until 2002; and Katon Kamp (1969–1972), which manufactured prefabricated homes. Phoenix Products, a kayak manufacturer, started up in 1973 in the old Tyner School then moved to Berea, Kentucky, in 1980. Tom Wilson, founder and owner of Phoenix, opened a new plant in Jackson County in 2003, producing kayaks and military helicopter parts. Phoenix employs about twenty people at the Northern Jackson County Industrial Park. Established in 1977, at Bond, was KMI (Kentucky Mountain Industries), a metal stamping company started by Jack Chestnut, an alumnus of Annville Institute. However, this company moved to Clay County in 1980.

For many years, Brockman Weavers made and sold hand-woven goods throughout the nation. Dorothy and Enos Brockman bought Campus Crafts (a student craft industry) from Annville Institute when it closed in 1978. In 1987, they changed the name to Brockman Weavers but continued to produce high-quality hand-woven goods until Mrs. Brockman's retirement in 1998.

In the mid 1980s, Jerry Weaver, a graduate of Annville Institute and owner of Mid-South Electrics, announced his intention to move his electronics and mechanical assembly company to Jackson County. Spurred by the opportunity to secure such a large-scale plant, local officials established the Jackson County/McKee Industrial Development Authority in November 1985. The mayor of McKee and the county judge appoint three members each to the Authority.

The Authority's first task was to accommodate the needs of Mid-South Electrics, including the securing of funds for a sewage treatment plant, water storage tank, and equipment loan money. Mid-South Electrics would buy the land and build the building.

President Bill Clinton visited Mid-South Electronics in 1999. He is shown here with Jerry Weaver, president of Mid-South, (in the white shirt) meeting employees. (Photograph by David Stephenson, *Lexington Herald-Leader*)

In 1987, Mid-South Electrics (later Electronics) dedicated a one hundred thousand square foot building at the newly established Jackson County Regional Industrial Park in Annville. The plant was a high-technology contract manufacturer of assemblies and subassemblies. Mid-South Electrics bought sixteen acres of land from the Industrial Authority and secured $4 million in bonds to build the building. They also committed to creating 350 new jobs. In 1992, Mid-South opened Plant 2, and, by 1993, employed over seven hundred people, with sales of over $80 million.

Expansion continued at the Industrial Park, with the opening of Phillips Diversified Manufacturing in 1993. The establishment of Jackson County as a federal Empowerment Zone in 1994, with its tax incentives, further spurred economic development. Several new businesses came to the county, including Image Entry (now SOURCECORP, Inc.), employing about thirty people in data processing; Stonewall Jackson Mold (now Annville Mold and Tool, a subsidiary of Mid-South Electronics), which builds molds and does machining; and Flat Rock Furniture, building high-end specialty furniture. JC TEC Industries, started by Judy Schmitt, opened in 1997 at the new Northern Jackson County Industrial Park. This company, which does molding assemblies and also builds portable furniture, is now located at the Annville Industrial Park.

In addition, the Empowerment Zone funded a "spec" building and started up the Jackson County Rehabilitation Industries (JCRI), a nonprofit effort to train workers in manufacturing. The JCRI Board secured its first contract to sew military hats at a building in Gray Hawk; then the company did some wood working at the old Tyner School before purchasing the spec building in the Industrial Park in Annville. In 1998, Jerry Weaver entered into a five-year management contract with JCRI, bringing in molding and assembly production. In 2003, JCRI was sold to Phillips Diversified and became a for-profit enterprise.

This is an aerial view of the Jackson County Regional Industrial Park in 2006. Plant 1 of Mid-South Electronics, in the foreground, was totally destroyed by fire in 2005. Other industries in the park include: Annville Mold and Tool, JC TEC Industries, Phillips Diversified Manufacturing, Source Corporation, and Plants 2, 3 and 4 of Mid-South Electronics, and the Annville Child and Development Center. (Courtesy of Jackson County EZ Community, Inc.)

A devastating fire in 2005 completely destroyed Mid-South's Plant 1. This was a severe blow, both to the company and the county. Nevertheless, the company continues to operate at the Industrial Park, employing about one hundred people at Plants 2 and 4.

Outside the three industrial parks are several other small manufacturing companies, including Gabbard's Sign Company, begun in 1971; Gatts & Company (1991), which makes forklift parts and does machining; Brewer's Truss Company (1994), which builds roof trusses; and Collin Manufacturing, a sewing enterprise begun in 2004.

This review of manufacturing industries in the county is brief and incomplete; but should give the reader a sense of the viability of this industry in rural areas such as Jackson County.

This 1900 photograph from the Southern Appalachian Archives in the Berea College Library is entitled, "Road to McKee." It looks like a very rough ride.

Transportation & Utilities

Connecting People & Places

*T*his chapter looks at the founding and growth of public and private services, including roads, railroads, electricity, telecommunications, and the county-wide water system.

ROADS

Long before the advent of the telegraph, telephone, or the electronic magic of the internet, roads and rivers provided the means of connecting people and places. To reach the land west of the Appalachian mountains, settlers used well-worn paths and trails—some made by Indians, some by the buffalo, and some by the European explorers. By 1858, when Jackson County was established, there were already many trails connecting the small communities which had sprung up during the early settlement of the area.

The importance of these "roads" is reflected in the recordings of the first county government. Among the first orders of business was the appointment of men to review various roads. Appointed in 1858 to review the road from McKee to the Estill County line were James Spyvy, David Goosey, and Levi Sparks. James Bales, Gotfrey Isaacs, and John Isaacks were to "review the road from McKee to the Madison County line and so with all roads leading out of McKee." (*Court Order Book 1*, 27)

Upon review, overseers were appointed to make improvements. For instance, a notation in the court's minutes from February 21, 1859, reads:

> Ordered that James Tincher be and he is hereby appointed overseer on the road leading from Traveller's Rest to the McKee and London Road ordered that he work from Pond Creek to the Laurel Fork of Rockcastle and he together with the hands allotted make the same agreeable to order. (Ibid., 92)

Thus, we learn that road construction and maintenance were the responsibility of the local citizens, and their compliance was apparently required by law. A court record of 1866 reads:

> It appearing to the Satisfaction of the Court that Aaron Faris is unable to perform labor on Public roads-it is ordered that he be exemt [sic] from working on roads forever after. (Ibid., 480)

This responsibility remained with local governments into the twentieth century, for it was not until 1912 that the State of Kentucky began appropriating aid for road construction in any meaningful way. (Raitz and O'Malley, 2004)

Still, roads were rough and suited only for horseback in many areas. Isaac Bowles described travel conditions in 1919:

> …horseback riding is the usual and practically the only method of travel, there being no automobiles and but few buggies in the county. This fact is no longer a mystery to the one who has traveled over these ungraded thoroughfares and seen that in many places the creek has broken from its natural course and follows the road bed for quite a

The Indian Creek bridge in McKee is shown here under construction in 1925. Prior to this construction, crossing the creek was a wet affair. (From the Fred De Jong Collection, courtesy of the De Jong family)

distance and usually the lowest place in the road is the center. The year 1919 seems to have been the real beginning of proper drainage of the roadbed. Possibly thirty percent of the roads were ditched on one or both sides and the center raised more or less so that the drain will be at the side rather than in the middle. A scarcity of bridges makes it impossible to cross the streams when they are flooded. There is only one large bridge (Flannery's bridge) in the county which will support the weight of a loaded wagon. (Bowles, [1919], 5)

Although the state began to assume responsibility for major roads in the early 1900s, county roads were still dependent upon "volunteers" for construction and maintenance as late as the 1930s. A notice in *The Jackson County Sun* in 1934 reads:

> To all Road Overseers of Jackson county: Notice is hereby given calling your attention to the fact that all males between the ages of 18 and 50 years, not exempt by law, must work on the public road six days a year. The road law has not changed. It is your duty to see that each and every hand works this full six days. if necessary to put and keep your section of road in repair. [This was signed by J. J. Davis Judge Jackson County Court.]

One of the first roads in the county to receive state attention was a road planned from Big Hill in Madison County passing through Jackson County to Manchester. It was to be called the Bosworth Trail and would connect Bradshaw, Gray Hawk, and Tyner with McKee—essentially the route of present day U.S. Highway 421. According to an article in *The Jackson County Sun,* it was built in sections from 1929 to 1936. The section from Big Hill to McKee was graveled in 1929, and the road completed in 1936.

The old Rockcastle River Railway bed was donated to the state about 1932, and construction making this a state road from East Bernstadt to Bond began in 1935 under the WPA (Works Progress Administration). The WPA also constructed (or reconstructed) the Sand Gap-Kerby Knob Road and the Foxtown Road.

The work of the Civilian Conservation Corps (CCC) during the 1930s, particularly in providing proper drainage, was beneficial to the improvement of several roads in the county. The CCC completely rebuilt what is now Kentucky Highway 89. Virgil Rose, who joined the CCCs when he was eighteen and lived in the McKee CCC camp, remembers:

> We worked mostly on the roads—built good roads where there were just wagon roads before—built 89

The Works Progress Administration (WPA) brought great improvement to many roads in Jackson County in the 1930s. Pictured here is the just completed Sand Gap-Kerby Knob Road. It is described as "graded and surfaced." (From the Goodman-Paxton Photographic Collection, 1934–1942 (Kukav64ml:638), University of Kentucky Archives)

In startling contrast to the 1900 "Road to McKee" is the 2007 road to McKee. (Photograph by Jean Fee)

down Indian Creek and worked on the bridge over South Fork. That bridge lasted until just a few years ago when it was replaced. They worked night and day—couldn't stop because of the cement—worked for nine days straight. I worked about two days on it and was rotated off. We camped right there—even had a cook. The cement was trucked in from Berea and the sand from Irvine. Most of the work was done by hand with a hand cement mixer—but it was good cement and built to last. The only machine was a little old grader.

Roads remain one of the most important functions of county, state, and federal governments. The rebuilding of the Big Hill Road (from Big Hill to Morrill) in 1999 was a major accomplishment. This was the first reconstruction work on this road since the completion of the Bosworth Trail in 1936. State Highway 30 is being rebuilt, with completion scheduled for 2010. And improvements to U.S. 421 are scheduled to begin in the near future.

RAILROADS

For a few years, there was a railroad in Jackson County. In 1913, the Rockcastle River Railway Company was established to provide a means to move timber from the Bond-Foley lumber mill to markets. Construction of the railroad began at East Bernstadt in December of 1913 and was completed to

Although the Rockcastle River Railway was built primarily to move lumber to market, it also carried passengers, as pictured in this photograph entitled: "First Train in Bond." Note the passenger carriage, just behind the engine. (Courtesy of Glennwood McQueen)

This scene of men "working on the railroad" is at the intersection of Gotfrey (now First Street) and Water Streets in McKee about 1925. Seen on the right is the roof of the jail, built in 1913; and on the left looking up Gotfrey Street are the old post office (later Holcomb's Drugstore) and Lloyd Sparks Store (the white building facing Wall (Main) Street). (From the Fred De Jong Collection, courtesy of the De Jong family)

Bond by September of 1914. Soon, the line was extended another ten miles to McKee and a little beyond. (Hudson 1996)

F. P. Dabolt served as vice president and general manager of the railroad. Roy E. Rader was general freight and passenger agent in 1914, later becoming assistant general manager of the Bond-Foley Lumber Company. Rader was instrumental in bringing to the county Robert Pearl, who was employed as treasurer of the railroad company. Pearl, although from a Catholic family, was instrumental in the beginnings of Bond Missionary Baptist Church. (Williams, 1995, 12, 14)

Most traffic on the railroad consisted of lumber and wood products, but the railway company maintained passenger service also, with formal time tables and schedules. Connections could be made in East Bernstadt to the L & N Railway going north and south. The train also provided a way to carry produce and animals to market—a much preferred alternative to wagons.

In the 1920s, the railroad handled an average of twenty-eight thousand tons of freight and over fourteen thousand passengers per year. (Hudson, 1996) By 1928, business had declined as the cutting of timber declined, and in 1930 the mill at Bond closed. The railroad was abandoned in 1932.

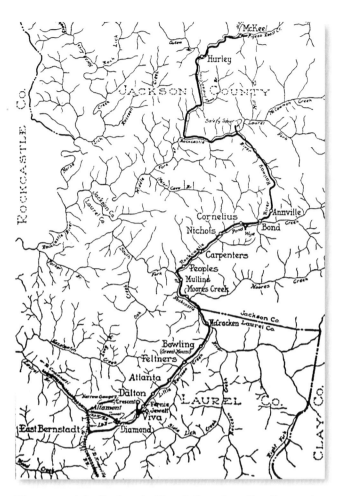

The route of the Rockcastle River Railway from East Bernstadt in Laurel County to McKee is shown in this map. (Reprinted from Hudson's *Jackson County, Kentucky; an Architectural History From an Appalachian Community*)

The right-of-way of the railroad was donated to the state of Kentucky, and with the help of the WPA (Works Progress Administration), Kentucky Highway 30 was begun in 1935.

ELECTRIC POWER

Electricity came to Jackson County in 1938 with the formation of a local cooperative. Like all electric cooperatives, Jackson Energy owes its beginning to President Franklin D. Roosevelt and the Rural Electrification Act of 1936. This act made low-cost loans available to nonprofit cooperatives, thus making electricity a real possibility for the ninety percent of Americans still without electricity.

The local cooperative was incorporated as Jackson County Rural Electric Cooperative Corporation (RECC) on July 28, 1938, during a meeting in the McKee Courthouse. The first directors were Coleman Reynolds, McKee,

Top left: Lester Reynolds, general manager, is shown in front of the Coop's first office in 1941. In 1950, a one-story brick building was built on the property, and a second story added in 1960. In 1980, the original house was moved across the street and still stands today opposite the PRTC Warehouse. (Courtesy of Jackson Energy)

Top right: The first electric pole in the county was set in 1939. Commemorating the event are, left to right, Bob Spence, J. A. Feltner, Fred De Jong, Walker Reynolds, Coleman Reynolds, Lloyd Sparks, Lester Reynolds, and Alfred Openeer. (Courtesy of Jackson Energy)

Above: Working on a substation in the 1940s are Willard Phelps and Russell Brewer. (Courtesy of Jackson Energy)

president; R. H. Johnson, Annville, vice president; D.G. Collier, McKee, secretary-treasurer; W. R. Feltner, Oneida; L. H. Sparks, McKee; J. R. Moberly, Oakley; and George Sparks, Eglon.

The directors borrowed $188,000 on December 27, 1938, to construct 131 miles of line in Clay, Jackson, Laurel, and Rockcastle Counties. The board minutes in 1939 mention progress on the project, but no specific date as to when the first members received service. By September 14, 1939, the minutes reported that 380 members were receiving service.

While Jackson County RECC crews constructed lines to serve the members, the power was purchased from an investor owned utility, Kentucky Utilities, and other electric cooperatives across the state were also purchasing power from privately-owned utilities.

In 1941, electric cooperatives took the first steps toward becoming self-sufficient. East Kentucky Power Cooperative was incorporated to provide electric power to thirteen cooperatives, including Jackson County RECC. Thus, the cooperatives, bound together in a larger unit, could control their own power generation plants and transmission lines.

Because of World War II, East Kentucky Power did not begin operation until 1951, when Jackson County RECC General Manager H. L. Spurlock was hired to head the organization located in Winchester, Kentucky.

From 380 members in 1939, Jackson Energy has grown with the region it serves. By 1971, there were 21,042 members served by 3,594 miles of line. That total doubled again by 1996 to 43,500 members and 5,081 miles of line.

To reflect the growth and development, the name of the cooperative was changed to Jackson Energy Cooperative in June 1997. In March 1998, Jackson Energy was among the first cooperatives in the country to become a Touchstone

Energy Partner, a national branding program promoting local electric cooperatives. Today, the cooperative serves over 51,000 members in fifteen counties of southeastern Kentucky and is headed by President & CEO Don Schaefer. He has held the post since 2000.

Although the number of members has risen since 1939, the electric cooperative's mission remains the same: to provide the modern infrastructure for the families and businesses making their homes in southeastern Kentucky.

Over the years, first as Jackson County RECC and then as Jackson Energy, the cooperative has had several managers and CEOs. They are: Ralph Skiff, 1939; A. S. Atwater, 1939–1940; Lester Reynolds, 1940–1941; James C. Roby, 1941–1942; James Jennings, 1942; Hugh Spurlock, 1943; Harry Tussey, 1943–1944; Moss Abshear, 1944–1946; Lester Reynolds, 1946–1947; Hugh Spurlock, 1947–1951; Luther Farmer, 1951–1974; Lee Roy Cole, 1974–1991; Doug Leary, 1991–2000; Don Schaefer, 2000 to present.

In 2001, Jackson Energy moved its headquarters out of McKee to KY Highway 290. The original property on Highway 421 was sold to the telephone cooperative, and a well-landscaped park and parking lot now occupy this space. (Photograph by Karen Combs)

TELEPHONE AND INTERNET SERVICE

One of the first telephone systems in the county was built by the Bond-Foley Lumber Company about 1916. This was a localized service, but the folks in Bond enjoyed this service until the mill shut down in 1930. The U.S. Forest Service also established a telephone system in the 1930s, connecting McKee to London. This was available to locals in emergencies.

A county-wide telephone service did not come into being until the 1950s, when members of the Jackson County Kiwanis Club spearheaded an effort to establish a local cooperative. Learning that low-interest loans for building a telephone system were available through the federal government, the club got busy; and soon a board of directors was formed, consisting of four men from Jackson County and three men from Owsley County. Articles of Incorporation were developed on November 30, 1950. The first board members were H. W. Tussey, R. Bruce Hays, Alfred Oppeneer, Jesse J. Smith, D. W. Barrett, Joe T. Morgan, and Pleas Turner. The first manager was Lyndon Anderson.

Pictured here is Charley Gray early in his career as an installer and repairman. Note the early name of the telephone co-op on the truck. Mr. Gray later served as general manager of the co-op. (Courtesy of PRTC)

The Peoples Rural Telephone Cooperative, known now simply as PRTC, became the first cooperative in the state of Kentucky to get a loan approved to construct a telephone system. They purchased the existing twenty-five phones in the forest service telephone system in 1951 and began operating out of a two-room office with four employees.

By the end of 1953, PRTC had 575 members and, by 1957, had opened a new office building in McKee. The cooperative continued to grow through the 1960s and 1970s. Bruce Hays, member and former president of the PRTC Board of Directors, was interviewed in 2007 and remembered:

The PRTC General Office, located on U.S. 421, was built in 1989. (Courtesy of PRTC)

> We started out on an eight-party line. When one person's phone would ring, everyone's phone in the county would ring. As we went into the 1960s, we dropped to six parties, then to four, and eventually we got down to two. In the late 1970s, we began to offer private lines, and in 1983, every PRTC customer had a single-party line.

Constructed in 2007, PRTC's Operations Building, which now centralizes the operations and IT (Information Technology) departments, sits on the bank of Pigeon Roost Creek, about a block from town center. (Photograph by Judy Schmitt)

In the 1980s and 1990s, PRTC joined the digital revolution, bringing customers a growing set of telecommunications options. With advanced services and features like call waiting, caller ID, and voice mail, customers could now personalize their service to meet their individual communication needs. The cooperative added cellular service in 1992 via Appalachian Wireless, and connected its customers to the World Wide Web in 1996. Long-distance from the local cooperative network was introduced in 2000, and high-speed internet service (DSL) was added in 2002. PRTC purchased its first cable television operation in 2005, with cable television service expanding each year. By 2006, broadband internet reached one hundred percent availability for its customers.

The cooperative's first headquarters was upstairs in an old frame building on the side of the RECC building. The cooperative's second home was the upstairs section of the old post office building on Gotfrey Street (later First Street), now part of the Jackson County Bank. In the late 1950s, PRTC bought the property occupied by a local Ford dealership and moved its headquarters there. PRTC moved to its current office on U.S. 421 South in

1989. In 2007, the co-op moved its operations and IT (information technology) departments into a new building just one block from town center.

PRTC has had four managers during its almost sixty-year history. Lyndon Anderson served as temporary manager until January 1953 and then as general manager until August 1954. Vee Gay, while serving as president of the PRTC Board of Directors, worked as advising manager from August 1954 until July 1955. He was then appointed general manager and served until his retirement in February 1977. Charley Gray followed Mr. Gay as general manager, serving until January 1996. Keith Gabbard was appointed general manager in January 1996 and still serves in that capacity in 2008. Peoples Rural Telephone Cooperative now serves over eight thousand customers in Jackson and Owsley Counties.

In an interview, Mr. Gabbard noted the loyalty and dedication of PRTC employees: "The Co-op would not be the success that it is without the support and loyalty of our employees. There have been many employees who have worked more than thirty years for the Cooperative."

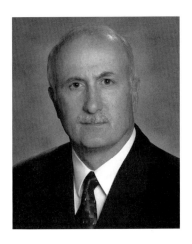

Pictured here are three of the four men who have served as general manager of the co-op over the years. Lyndon Anderson, who served from 1953–1954 is not pictured.

Top left: Vee Gay, 1954–1977.
Top right: Charley Gray, 1977–1996.
Above: Keith Gabbard, 1996–present.

And Cozette Neeley, who has been with the Cooperative for almost forty years and is now PRTC's information systems manager, comments: "PRTC has never stopped moving forward and has worked hard to bring service to as many people as possible and then to give our customers more choices."

COUNTY WATER SYSTEM

In the late 1960s, the state of Kentucky, under the administration of Governor Louis Nunn, constructed a ninety-acre water supply reservoir at Tyner. It was named for the governor's wife, Beulah, whose family had roots in Jackson County. The reservoir made possible the establishment of a county-wide water distribution system. In 1969, the Jackson County Water Association was established to build a water treatment and supply system. Wendell Flannery was elected chairman; Odis Johnson, vice chairman; and Alfred May, secretary-treasurer.

In 1973, with a combination of grant and loan monies, 43.8 miles of water lines were laid in the areas of Sand Gap, Waneta, Bradshaw, Gray Hawk, Tyner, and Annville, serving 518 customers. A water treatment plant was completed in the same year. Additional water lines were laid in 1979, 1986, 1991, 1995, and 1997. Today, with a new treatment plant completed in 2005, the Association serves 4,500 customers.

This picture was entitled, "The Moores Creek Mob" and dated 1915. Is it a church organization or just a picture with an intriguing caption? Pictured left to right standing are Luther Boggs, Steve Baldwin, Cyrus (last name unreadable), Frank Morris, Dillard Moore, and Walter Dyche. Seated left to right are James P. King, Green Gabbard, Bob Dyche, George Moore, and Leonard Moore. (Courtesy of Mary Moore)

Clubs *&* Organizations

*A*mericans of all ages, all conditions and all dispositions, constantly form associations. They have not only commercial and manufacturing companies, in which all take part, but associations of a thousand other kinds—religious, moral, serious, futile, extensive, or restricted, enormous or diminutive.

Democracy in America, Alexis de Tocqueville, 1845—Chapter 5, "Of the Use Which the Americans Make of Public Associations in Civil Life."

Jackson County is no exception to the observation above. Clubs and organizations have formed, disbanded, and formed again—ever-changing, but ever-sustaining. For instance, there was the Moores Creek Mob. It is thought that this group of young (and not so young) men came together as a fellowship group affiliated with Cornett's Chapel Christian Church. However, it may be that someone just penned "Moores Creek Mob" on this picture and there was no formal organization.

And then there was once the Pollyanna Club. (See picture on page 125.) In the late 1960s, a group of women gathered at Ruth Hall's home to help with a quilt, but found they wanted to keep meeting together. Violet Allen suggested that they make quilts for those in need and call themselves the Pollyanna Club, after the story of a young girl who always sees the good in life and who wants to bring gladness into the lives of others. These ladies made quilts to raise money for those in need or to give to those in need. They quilted for over five years before illness called a halt for several members. The last quilt they made was donated to the Pond Creek Fire Department.

Top: The Masons have been active in the county for many years. Pictured here is a typical Masonic funeral in 1935. Only a few of these mourners have been identified. They are George Seals on the far left with Tilman Seals and Bob Johnson just below him on the left of the coffin, and on the far right is Asa Cornelius. (Courtesy of Lorene Adkins)

Above: The McKee Boy Scouts were very active in the 1950s. Shown here at the home of Scout Leader, Jeff Boggs, are, standing, left to right: Paul Sears, Fred Lakes, Bruce Boggs (in the truck), William "Tom" Thomas, and Cordell Huff; kneeling, left to right: Lewis Ray Norris, Billie Sears, Lee Dorse Dunsil, and Leroy Morris. (Courtesy of Paul Sears)

Among church women's social groups was "King's Daughters," a group within the Reformed Church. Two such groups are pictured on the right.

Boy Scout and Girl Scout troops have been formed at various times in the county. And special interest groups, such as the Beekeepers Association, or the Cattlemen's Association, are active. Among such organizations with an agricultural theme is Heifer International, of which the local Chain of Life organization, created in 1984, is affiliated. Heifer International was organized in 1944 to send animals (usually heifers), instead of relief money, to people in need.

The Jackson County Women's Club, affiliated with the Kentucky Federation of Women's Clubs, was very active for a time. Members included Jean Llewellyn, Bonnie Whicker, Margaret Rader, Evelyn Sinclair, Bessie Kerns, Sue Hignite, and Evelyn Hays, among others. A special remembrance of this club is the play performed in 1973 called "Mountain Gal." This production was sponsored by both the Women's Club and the Jackson County Jaycees. Pictured on page 126 is the cast of that event. The Women's Club also held the first radio auction in the county in order to raise funds to furnish the kitchen of the new Community Center, which was built in the early 1970s by the Women's Club and the Kiwanis Club. The Community Center operated only a few years before being sold to the Jackson County Board of Education in 1974. The Board still occupies this building.

The Masons have had a long history in Jackson County and, in 1983, dedicated a new Masonic Temple. Nearby is a picture of a Masonic funeral in 1935.

Above: Pictured here about 1937 are the ladies of the Gray Hawk Reformed Church, belonging to an organization called "King's Daughters." Back Row, left to right are: Ruby Hays, unidentified, Nora Edwards, unidentified, Effie Kelley, Janie Bennett, Janie Hays, Mable Farmer, Lou Morris, Martha McGeorge, Mattie Hunter, Ersie Judd, Rhoda Shepherd, Dena Kots. Seated in front are: Rosa Robinson, Salomi Turner, Dorothy Tanis, Rosa Bennett, Della Pennington, and Rhoda Edwards. (Courtesy of Carroll De Forest)

Middle: The King's Daughters of Annville Reformed Church are here dressed up in old-fashioned costume for a day of fun. (Courtesy of Mary Moore)

Bottom: The Pollyanna Quilting Club is shown here in the 1960s. Pictured left to right are Becky Wilson, Ruth Hall, Maude Wilson, Eliza Rader, Laura Evans, Violet Allen, Laura Johnson, Cornelia Mathis, Becky Moore, Emma Webb, Ida Estridge, and Vada Frazier. (Courtesy of Violet Allen)

In 1973, the Jackson County Women's Club and the Jackson County Jaycees staged a production of "Mountain Gal," much to the enjoyment of all. The cast is pictured here, left to right: Melvin "Blue" Lakes, Sue Hignite, Auriel Aalberts, John Smith, Jim Griffith, Joan Laudati, Bonnie Whicker, Jim Potts, Margaret Rader, and Bill Moore. (Courtesy of Margaret Rader)

The first radio auction in the county was held by the Women's Club in the early 1970s to raise money to furnish the kitchen for the new Community Center. Pictured left to right are: Viola Bingham, Margaret Rader, and Mable Farmer. The Jackson County Board of Education now occupies the old Community Center at the corner of U.S. 421 and McCammon Ridge Road. (Courtesy of Margaret Rader)

Receiving the national "Passing of the Gift" Award, in 1988, from Heifer International's Steve Muntz, are James "Buster" and Juanitta Welborn, leaders in Jackson County's Chain of Life organization. Standing at the left, next to Buster are board members Hiram Whitaker and Arvel Evans. At the far right is Jeff Henderson, Jackson County Agricultural Extension Agent. (Courtesy of the Jackson County Extension Service)

Enjoying a day of visiting and whittling at the Standafer War Memorial at Sand Gap are, left to right, Darrell Baker, Burley Rose, Bill Nichols, and Lloyd Lakes, members of the "Sand Gap Whittlers." (Photograph by George Ferrell)

And lately, there has formed a group of men who meet just about every day at the Standafer War Memorial at Sand Gap—they call themselves "The Sand Gap Whittlers."

Following is a look at a few other organizations in the county.

THE KIWANIS CLUB

The Kiwanis Club is an international service organization which had its beginnings in Detroit, Michigan, in 1915. Although originally a men's club formed for fellowship and community service, Kiwanis opened its doors to women in 1987. The name, Kiwanis, is from an American Indian language of the Detroit area meaning "We Trade" or "We Share Our Talents."

According to a history of the local club, written by Reverend Fred H. De Jong in 1944, the Jackson County Kiwanis Club was formed in 1938 with the recruitment of twenty-five men from six communities within the county.

These men represented McKee, Annville, Tyner, Sand Gap, Gray Hawk, and Eberle. The first officers were Coleman Reynolds, president; Thomas Dunigan, vice president; and Edward Hays, secretary-treasurer. The first board of directors consisted of W. R. Reynolds, J. R. Hays, Alfred Oppeneer, Reverend George T. Kots, Farris Morris, Reverend W. A. Worthington, and C. P. Moore.

The club adopted as its main project for 1938 the organization of an electric cooperative in the county. Kiwanians who incorporated or were on the first board of directors of the Jackson County Rural Electric Cooperative were Coleman Reynolds, D. G. Collier, and L. H. Sparks.

The Jackson County Kiwanis Club hosts the annual Doug Rader Memorial Golf Scramble, a fundraiser for maintenance of Bond Memorial Park. The 1999 winners, shown left to right, are Chris Boggs, Ricky Joe Boggs, Jeff Henderson, Owen Collins, Becky Leary, and Keith Hays. (Courtesy of the Jackson County Extension Service)

The Kiwanis Club was also instrumental in the founding of the local telephone cooperative in the 1950s.

After the dissolution of the CCC camp in McKee in the 1940s, N. U. Bond donated this land to the Kiwanis Club to be used as a community park. Over the years, Kiwanians have developed Bond Memorial Park so that it now contains a baseball field, basketball court, children's playground, and two shelters for community picnics and events. The Little League program is the major focus of the local club, providing recreation and fun for the entire county. The

Huda Jones, a Jackson County native and the first vice-president of the National Federation of Republican Women in 1988, is shown here with President George H. W. Bush. Mrs. Jones was a 1955 graduate of Tyner High School and was Miss Jackson County RECC in 1956. She resides in Beattyville, Kentucky, today. (Courtesy of Huda Jones)

upkeep of the park is supported by various fundraising traditions, including the Kiwanis Radio/TV Auction, held every year in February, and the Doug Rader Memorial Golf Scramble, held every summer.

In addition, the Kiwanis Club sponsors the Homecoming Parade held each year on the Saturday before Labor Day.

THE REPUBLICAN WOMEN'S CLUB

The Jackson County Republican Women's Club has been active since at least the 1950s. So active, in fact, that, in the late 1950s, the local president, Nola Gay, was elected as the state president. The club holds an annual Lincoln Day Dinner as a fund raiser to promote local, regional, and state candidates.

The local club is also affiliated with the National Federation of Republican Women. And another native daughter, Huda Jones, was elected the at-large representative of this national organization in 1973. Mrs. Jones was elected president of the Federation in 1989 and again in 1991.

Jackson County has long been a Republican stronghold. In an article in the *Courier-Journal* on April 7, 1961, by Harvey L. Carter, Jackson County was named the most Republican county in the United States. From 1868 to 1960, over eighty-six percent of the vote in presidential elections in Jackson County went to the Republican candidate. In 2007, only twelve percent of registered voters in Jackson County were registered Democrat and eighty-six percent were registered Republican. It is no surprise that there is not a Democrat Women's Club in the county.

THE JACKSON COUNTY DEVELOPMENT ASSOCIATION

The Jackson County Development Association, established in 1984, is not the first citizens group to organize for community development, although it may be among the most long-lasting. Earlier development organizations included a Jackson County Development Association, which built a medical clinic in 1960, and a Jackson County Betterment, Improvement, and Development Association (1963), whose efforts led to the establishment of a central land-fill in the county. Citizens involved in this project included Harry Wilson, Alfred Isaacs, James R. Hays, Margie Hillard, and Zenas York. (*The Jackson County Sun*, January 3, 1963, and June 15, 1963)

Like its predecessors, the Jackson County Development Association of 1984 was formed by local citizens who perceived the need to improve opportunities and the quality of life within the county. Among these first members were

Lowell Wagner, Jeff Henderson, Marie Rader, Jack Gabbard, Judy Schmitt, William Smith, Beulah Venable, Lewis Ray Norris, and Gene Hensley. The original focus for the group was the promotion of tourism and recreation. Many ideas were discussed and some feasibility studies conducted. Among them were proposals for a lake, an airport, and a golf course. But the first major accomplishment was the location in the county of Mid-South Electrics, Inc. The Association organized public meetings and put together a successful proposal. Mid-South remained a major employer until 2005 when a fire, combined with pressures from off-shore competition, greatly diminished the work force.

Other accomplishments of the Development Association have included the development of a strategic plan for economic and community development, most recently updated in 2002; the establishment of mandatory garbage collection; and the Big Hill road improvements. A most successful project of the Development Association was an annual Memorial Day festival called the "Jackson County Rondayvoo." Started in 1985, the festival continued for about ten years. In 2007, the Association undertook the publication of this pictorial history of Jackson County.

HOMEMAKERS AND 4-H CLUBS

The Jackson County Cooperative Extension Service, operated by the University of Kentucky, is the parent organization for two popular clubs in the county: Extension Homemaker Clubs and 4-H Clubs. Both of these clubs have been in existence for many years in Jackson County.

The Homemaker's Scrappy Quilter's Club is shown busily working on a quilt in 1999. Pictured, left to right, are Irene Moore, Darlene Martin, Pauline Powell, and Eula Jackson. (Courtesy of the Jackson County Extension Service)

Homemakers

The Jackson County Extension Homemaker Clubs came about as part of the Home Demonstration Agent's job to "extend to homemakers the opportunity to study homemaking problems under trained leadership, to increase their skill, add to their information, develop their knowledge to the end that they may apply their contributions of science and art in their homes and may more effectively contribute to the well-being of their communities."

The first Extension Homemaker Clubs in Kentucky were established in the late 1920s in Harlan County, but had to wait until 1959 in Jackson County, when the first Home Demonstration Agent, Margaret Hatfield Rader, was hired. Mrs. Rader started several clubs during her tenure in the county, including McKee, Moores Creek, Sand Gap, and Tyner. And in the early 1960s, Jackson County Homemakers joined the Kentucky Federation of Homemakers, later to become the Kentucky Extension Homemakers Association.

Over the years, additional groups were organized, including Seven Pines, Indian Creek, Morrill, Three Links, Annville, Above Ruby's, Egypt, Gray Hawk, Heart of the County, McKee Manor, Cross Creek, Scrappy Quilters, and the expansion of the Sand Gap Club to include Northern Jackson County. Many of these clubs are still active today.

The Jackson County Homemakers do far more than just sew, quilt, cook, and make crafts. They are very interested in community service and have worked hard throughout the years to help the citizens of this county. They have sponsored blood drives, environmental and recycling programs, summer reading programs, fair exhibits, and International Dinners just to name a few of their projects.

Pictured here is a local 4-H gathering in the 1920s. Although the 4-H Club of Jackson County has a long history, it was not until 1979 that the county hired its first 4-H Agent, Lowell Wagner. (From the Fred De Jong Collection, courtesy of the De Jong family)

4-H Clubs

In 1914, when the Cooperative Extension Service was established, the County Agriculture Agents and Home Demonstration Agents provided the professional staff and support needed to direct the growth of the early 4-H programs. 4-H's goal was to teach youth to "learn by doing." In the name 4-H, the H's signify Head, Heart, Hands, and Health.

In Jackson County, Walker Rexford Reynolds began as the county agriculture agent in 1914. Extension records report that Mr. Reynolds put the most emphasis on the youth of the county. He started pig and corn clubs that were the forerunners of 4-H clubs in the county.

From these beginnings, 4-H has had a long, strong history in Jackson County. In 1963, there were twenty-five schools in Jackson County, with 2,578 students eligible to be involved in 4-H clubs. Twenty-five percent (645 students) were 4-H members in the county. 4-H clubs were and still are open to youth in the county between the ages of nine to nineteen years old.

As the program continued to grow, interested parents and volunteers saw a need for more help with the Jackson County 4-H Program. Ruby Tincher, a long-time 4-H volunteer, recalled, in an interview shortly before her death in 2008: "At all the Area Extension Service meetings, we told everyone that would listen that we needed our own 4-H Agent." Finally, in 1979, Lowell Wagner was hired as the first 4-H/Youth Development Agent in the county. Under Wagner's leadership, the club focused primarily on environmental education and leadership development.

4-H clubs continue to be a part of Jackson County. There are school clubs and after-school specialty clubs, an annual Speech & Demonstration Contest, and a Variety and Talent Show. In addition, members enter exhibits during the Jackson County Fair.

The annual Homecoming Parade, sponsored by the Kiwanis Club, is a very popular event. Held on the Saturday before Labor Day, the parade is larger each year, with floats, antique cars, horseback riders, four-wheelers, and marchers. (Courtesy of Judy Wilson)

Festivals & Fun Times

$\mathcal{F}$rom the harvest festivals of ancient times, to the medieval fairs of England, to the American state fairs of today, mankind has always found reason to celebrate. It is likely that our American county fairs had their roots in medieval England, where fairs were important places for commerce and also provided entertainment with clowns, acrobats, and plays. Although we no longer barter and trade farm products, we celebrate the farm and the bounty of the harvest; and we most certainly look forward to the ferris wheel and clowns.

But people do not need formal events to celebrate life. Family gatherings on Sunday afternoons, schoolyard games, picnics in the park, or boating on the river—all lend credence to the human need to lay down the load of work for a little while.

This chapter highlights some of the fairs and festivals that have come and gone over 150 years and also depicts people at play in photographs that have been collected for this book.

JACKSON COUNTY FAIR AND HOMECOMING

County fairs are an American tradition and have been a tradition in Jackson County since at least 1915. Isaac Bowles, in his manuscript, *History of Jackson County, Kentucky,* states that the county fair developed from a school fair held in October of 1915. This was so successful that, the next year, exhibits of farm and home products were included:

> A plantation show was added with all its charms. Fine horses, cattle, hogs, prize sheep and chickens were on exhibition. The courthouse and

County fairs have been a part of Jackson County's history for many years. The Bond/Annville Fairgrounds pictured here was one of the largest and best known of its day. The date of this picture is thought to be in the 1920s, but perhaps it is earlier—note the uniformed men seen strolling in the right foreground. (From the Anna Blair Collection, courtesy of JoAnne Blair Moore)

lot were used this time but [in] 1917 land was purchased at Annville and some buildings erected and a permanent county fair was organized. The fairs of 1917, '18, and '19 were very successful and so well-attended that the stockholders in the organization received good dividends. (p.8)

The next documentation of a county fair was found in an article in *The Jackson County Sun* in 1929, announcing plans for a fair to be held September 5–7. The paper announces that it will "print the catalogue and other advertising matter,"—a tradition carried forth today by *The Jackson County Sun*.

In another article just prior to the 1929 fair, which featured a high-wire act and "the best band in Kentucky," the paper states:

It is generally understood that this Fair is one of the best in Kentucky. It is here where thousands of mountain people meet annually for a HOME COMING and a good time. Since the construction of the Bosworth Trail and other good roads in the Mountains, it is easy for our Blue Grass friends to come and be with us mountain people.

Since then, the Jackson County Fair and Homecoming has continued—sometimes large and sometimes small. And although recent fairs haven't featured acrobats on a high wire, they remain a favorite end-of-summer event. Of special enjoyment is the Homecoming Parade sponsored by the Kiwanis Club each year on the Saturday before Labor Day. And not to be overlooked is the beauty pageant, whose winners always ride in the parade.

RONDAYVOO

A celebration called the Jackson County Rondayvoo began in 1985, sponsored by the Development Association. This event was held to celebrate the heritage and customs of the community and featured games, story-telling, and exhibitions of local artisans and artists. This event continued annually for about ten years.

STRINGBEAN BLUEGRASS MUSIC FESTIVAL

In 1996, Phillip Akemon and his family staged the first "Stringbean" Bluegrass Music Festival to honor his late uncle, David "Stringbean" Akemon, who died a victim of murder and robbery in 1973. Many still remember "Stringbean" as the long and lanky banjo musician and mainstay of the television program "Hee Haw," which was popular throughout the 1970s and into the 80s.

This event is held annually at the Stringbean Memorial Music Park near Gray Hawk and has featured such notable country stars as Grandpa Jones, Porter Wagoner, and Ralph Stanley. In addition, local talent is given the opportunity to perform; and Phillip Akemon has used the festival to educate local school children in the heritage of bluegrass music.

Top left: Tobacco, once a mainstay of the local economy, is also a source of good-natured rivalry during the Jackson County Fair. Seen here are the winners of the 1999 contest: (left to right) Mark Lewis, Anthony Tillery, Roger Brewer, Jonathon Jackson, Robert Adkins, and Willie Ray Hubbard. (Photograph by George Ferrell)

Top right: The 2007 Jackson County Homecoming Parade featured Governor Ernie Fletcher and First Lady Glenna Fletcher, shown here riding in a vintage automobile. (Photograph by George Ferrell)

Above: A popular folk festival held from 1985–1995, "Rondayvoo" featured demonstrations and exhibits of life in long ago days. Pictured here is Winston Holt from Berea, sampling some of his campfire cooking. (Photograph by George Ferrell)

Grandpa Jones of stage and television fame, pictured here with McKee Mayor Jack Gabbard, attended the 1990 Rondayvoo. (Courtesy of Keith Gabbard)

Famed singer, Porter Wagoner, is seen here signing autographs at the Stringbean Memorial Music Park in 1996. David "Stringbean" Akemon, of Grand Ole Opry renown and a star of the hit television show "Hee Haw," is one of Jackson County's famous sons. An annual music festival is held in his honor at the park and memorial which were established by his nephew Phillip Akemon. (Courtesy of Beulah Venable)

MUNCY PARK GOSPEL SINGING

While living and working in Dayton, Ohio, Jim Muncy and friends, Archie Lunsford and Darrel Webb, talked often about coming down to Jim's home and putting on a gospel singing. And in 1974, that dream became a reality with the first Jackson County Gospel Singing, held at the Shepherd Park at Mildred. This three-day event continued there for nine years and then moved to the newly constructed Muncy Park, where it is currently held each year on the fourth weekend in June.

Coming back each year to sing is Darrel Webb, and occasionally Archie Lunsford returns. Over the years, the event has drawn national attention with performances from groups, such as The Singing Cooks, The Primitive Quartet, and The Spencers. Local groups also perform, including The Smith Sisters, The Combs Family, and The Christian Echoes. Favorite performers also include Blue Lakes and Gary Gay.

Jim Muncy, who returned to the county in 1987, says that he really enjoys doing this: "We hope to continue for years to come."

YOUTH FEST

The youth of Sand Gap Christian Church host the Youth Fest each Fall at the Sand Gap Park. The two-night event, known for good gospel music, draws a crowd of a thousand or more each year.

BETHEL HOMECOMING

In 1994, the first annual Bethel Homecoming was held at the newly renovated Bethel Baptist Church in the Horse Lick area. Renovation of the old church building was spearheaded by local businessman Murrell Lakes and financed jointly by the descendants of the early members and The Nature Conservancy, with special help from Mr. Lakes. From its beginning, this celebration has been a county-wide event—open to all who want to bring a dish for "dinner on the ground" and enjoy some good eating, visiting, and gospel singing.

Marie Lakes Rader, Murrell's sister and State Representative from the 89th District, was born on Horse Lick at the small community of Loam. Her father, Bart Lakes, also born there, was the eldest of nine children. He grew up there, married, and brought his wife, Maggie Morris Lakes, home to begin raising a family. Marie shares her memories of family stories:

> It was quite a settlement at one time, with a school, church, grocery store, and a post office— it was a gathering place for the many farming families in the area.
>
> When my dad was a young man, he left to work in Cincinnati. He sent money home so that his younger siblings could go on to high school. He had only finished the eighth grade. The only way to get a high school education in those days was to go to boarding school, since there wasn't a high school close enough to walk to. And three of them did go to the Annville Institute: Ed, Hillard, and Evelyn.
>
> Later, Dad came back, married and began to raise a family. He and my mother ran a grocery store. He had one of the earliest vehicles in the county and would carry out the eggs and milk and such that had been traded at the store for goods, and bring back other goods to sell or trade at the store.

Murrell Lakes told *The Jackson County Sun* in an interview in 1994 about the difficulty getting in and out of the isolated valley: "The roadway coming in may have been one reason the town never flourished—rocky, steep, gullied and crossing a creek twice. They used to use wagon and mules and parked at the top of the hill. In the early 50s, late 40s, people moved."

The Bethel Homecoming is held the third Sunday in September.

Bethel Homecoming has been a popular annual event since 1994, featuring gospel singing and "dinner-on-the-ground." The renovated Bethel Church is seen here in the background with revelers enjoying good food and good company in 1998. (Courtesy of the Jackson County EZ Community, Inc.)

Life in the Bethel community on Horse Lick did not include the luxury of a secondary education in the early 1900s. This could only be obtained by boarding at Annville or McKee. Bart Lakes, pictured here in Cincinnati in 1928, went off to the big city in order to earn enough money for three of his younger siblings to attend boarding school. (Courtesy of Marie Lakes Rader)

HORSE LICK CREEK BIORESERVE

■ ■ ■

Established in 1993 and named for the creek which drains the area, this reserve encompasses over forty thousand acres in Jackson and Rockcastle Counties. The Nature Conservancy, the U.S. Forest Service, and private landowners not only share ownership, but also a sense of responsibility for the protection and management of this special place. The area is abundant in native flora and fauna—in spite of many years of human habitation—and is managed cooperatively by the U.S. Forest Service, The Nature Conservancy, the Kentucky State Nature Preserves Commission, Jackson County, and the Kentucky Department of Fish and Wildlife Resources. The region was designated one of "America's Last Great Places" by The Nature Conservancy in 1992.

Cars were scarce in 1919, but couples like Winfred Van Winkle and Elva Eversole were in fine courting style in this buggy. (Courtesy of Wanda Renner)

Sunday afternoons were, and sometimes still are, a time for families and friends to get together for conversation and news-sharing. Seen here enjoying one of these moments are, left to right: Martha Pigg Turner, Martha Fields, unknown, Bob Turner, and Nathan Fields. (Courtesy of Judy Wilson)

Pictured in front of his recreated 1930s garage, is Travis Sparks in 2007. For fifteen years, Mr. Sparks has been building a vintage village of the 1920s–30s. Oakwood Acres now boasts a country store, a typical dwelling of the era, a school house, as well as the garage and filling station. (Photograph by Fletcher Gabbard)

Ralph Marcum stands in front of the old mill at Hooten Old Town, a recreated frontier town. The Single Action Shooting Society, an organization formed to promote and preserve the history of the Old West and competitive shooting, meets monthly at Hooten Old Town. (Photograph by Fletcher Gabbard)

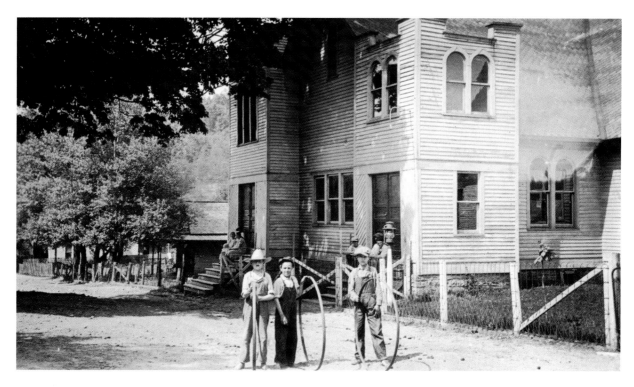

Toys in the 1920s were usually fairly simple, but the company of some friends made it all great fun, as shown by the hoopsters in front of the McKee Reformed Church. (From the Fred De Jong Collection, courtesy of the De Jong family)

Horses and mules, always associated with Kentucky life, provided not only a work source, but also a fun day of pleasure riding. Pictured here are Albert McGee and Herman Carpenter sometime in the early 1900s. (Courtesy of Glenna Carpenter)

Children, then as now, found pets a source of amusement. Pictured on a rock above their grandparents farm are, left to right, Jack Flannery and his dog Fannie, Lavelle Flannery, holding a pet chicken, and Jean Van Winkle with her dog. (Courtesy of Wanda Renner)

This group of students from McKee, shown at the John S. and Annis Lakes house in the 1920s, are loaded up and headed out for a fine time at Wind Cave. Pictured on the porch is Luther Lakes, and the little boy at the post is Floyd Isaacs. On horseback are teachers, Miss Sywassink and Miss Whiteveck. (From the Fred De Jong Collection, courtesy of the De Jong family)

A picnic outing provided a day of play and outdoor adventure for this group shown posing on a foot log across Indian Creek in 1925. (From the Fred De Jong Collection, courtesy of the De Jong family)

Alpha Gay enjoys a day of roller skating on the new sidewalk around the Jackson County Courthouse. This was a sport not possible until sidewalks were built in the early 1930s. (Courtesy of Jack Norris)

Coon-hunting was a mountain tradition and an excellent way for men to gather and enjoy conversation and camaraderie. The possession of a good coon dog was a source of much pride. Charlie Lakes is shown here holding the coon which he and his hound, Dino, have just vanquished. (Courtesy of Bobby Lakes)

Angling is a sport and pastime enjoyed by children and adults alike. A boat, like this one used by Ray Hornsby on Laurel Fork, can provide access to excellent fishing venues. (From the Engle Collection, courtesy of Ginny Ashonosheni)

Jane, Zenas, and Glenna York are showing off some Sunday clothes and great pride in the play wagon made by their father, Delbert York. (Courtesy of Glenna Carpenter)

This picture, taken in 1924, shows friends enjoying an outing to the Pretty House, a favorite cliff formation near Wind Cave. The lady seated in the foreground on the left is Clara Lakes Richardson. The other two seated ladies are unidentified. Seated at the left rear are John Maupin, Gracie Brewer, holding Clyde Brewer, and Charlotte Lakes. Standing are Anna May and Elby Maupin, and Lloyd Lakes. (Courtesy of Dewey Brewer)

Flat Lick Falls, then as now, is a favorite place for picnicking, splashing in the water, and just plain enjoying one of nature's last great places. In 2007 the Jackson County government purchased this scenic wonder to be preserved as a public park. These out-of-season visitors in 1925 are unidentified. (From the Fred De Jong Collection, courtesy of the De Jong family)

Enjoying a horseback ride on Gotfrey Street and posed in front of the McKee Reformed Church are Geraldine Hays, Christine Hays, and Thelma Baker. (Courtesy of James Earl Hays)

Singing, whether in church or at social gatherings, was and is, a much-enjoyed activity in eastern Kentucky. Posing here is the Annville Baptist Church singing group about 1943, composed of Earl Smith, Glenna York, June Turner, Lloyd Rader, and Walker House. (Courtesy of Glenna Carpenter)

A wagon load of sight-seers poses here at Gay's Store at Foxtown in 1925. (From the Fred De Jong Collection, courtesy of the De Jong family)

Pictured here about 1925 are students from the McKee Academy, enjoying an outing to the Birch Lick lumber camp. The camp was located at Elisha Branch, where the train turned around. Standing in the doorway is the camp cook. (From the Fred DeJong Collection, courtesy of the De Jong family)

A homemade paddle boat provides lots of fun on Grassy in 1939. Clyde Bingham is paddling the boat, which was built by Green Wright. Seated behind Clyde is Elsie Bingham and standing beside her is Fred Bingham. The children in the background, to the left of Fred Bingham, are, left to right, Evelyn Bingham, George Bingham, Dank Bingham, Earl Hurst, unknown, William Bingham, Thelma Bingham, and Wendell Bingham. To the right of Fred are Carmen and Reba Bingham. Seated at left on the bank is Walter Bingham. (Courtesy of Mary Coffey)

Picnics are a universal form of recreation. Pictured here in 1945 are, seated left to right, Katherine Turner and Nora Lee York. The only others identified are Johnny Cody, standing with sweater on, and Irene Fields, standing with long-sleeve white blouse on. (Courtesy of Glenna Carpenter)

145

World War II servicemen home on leave are pictured here left to right; Earl Van Winkle, Dewey Abrams, and Arnold Abrams. (Courtesy of Wanda Renner)

Wars

The impact of our country's wars on families and communities can range from little involvement by the general public (as with the conflict in Iraq, where only the families of the military are asked to sacrifice) to the every day, every hour, inescapable awareness of war and all that it means (as in World War II). In our story of Jackson County, we now take a look at the wars of American involvement since the founding of the county in 1858 and their effect on the county and its people.

Omitted from this discussion are the Gulf War (1990–1991) and the ongoing Global War on Terrorism, which began in 2003. These we leave for comment by future historians. This chapter is dedicated to the many brave soldiers from Jackson County who served, fought, and died for their country.

THE CIVIL WAR

The Civil War was the most devastating war in the history of the United States, claiming over six hundred thousand lives. Kentucky remained neutral in this struggle, but not without division between sections of the state, between families, and within families. Thomas Clark, in his *History of Kentucky,* emphasizes this:

> Families were divided with brother fighting brother and father fighting son. The Reverend Robert J. Breckinridge had two sons in the Confederate Army and two in the Union Army. Civil officials elected on the same ticket and of the same political opinions joined opposing forces. Members of the same denominations were sharply divided in their attitudes. (Clark, 1960, 315)

Perhaps it was fitting that Kentucky remained neutral. Both Abraham Lincoln, president of the United States and leader of the Union forces, and Jefferson Davis, president of the Confederacy, were native sons of Kentucky. And both leaders demanded troops from Kentucky, with 103,000 men responding for the Union and 35,000 to 40,000 for the Confederates. About 25,000 of the total Union troops from Kentucky were African-American. Kentucky also supplied sixty-seven natives or residents who were generals for the Union and thirty-eight natives or residents as generals for the Confederates. (Hutchinson, 1965)

The people of the Kentucky mountains were overwhelmingly loyal to the Union—as were the Southern Appalachian people in general. William G. Frost, president of Berea College (1892–1920), is quoted in Kephart's *Our Southern Highlanders*:

> The loyalty of this region in the Civil War was a surprise to both northern and southern statesmen. The mountain people owned land but did not own slaves, and the national feeling of the revolutionary period had not spent its force among them. (Kephart, 1913, Rev. ed. 1976, 449)

Likewise, the writer, John Fox Jr., also quoted in Kephart's work, says:

> …Confederate leaders were counting on the presumption that Mason and Dixon's Line was the dividing line between the North and South, and formed, therefore, the plan of marching an army from Wheeling in West Virginia, to some point on the Lakes, and thus dissevering the North at one blow. …[W]hen [Garnett] struck the mountains, he struck enemies who shot at his men from ambush … and Garnett himself fell with a bullet from a mountaineer's squirrel rifle at Harper's Ferry.
>
> Then the South began to realize what a long, lean, powerful arm of the Union it was that the southern mountaineer stretched through its very vitals; for that arm helped hold Kentucky in the Union by giving pre-ponderance to the Union sympathizers in the Bluegrass. …it drew out a horde of one hundred thousand volunteers, when Lincoln called for troops, depleting Jackson County, Kentucky, for instance, of every male under sixty years of age and over fifteen; and it raised a hostile barrier between the armies of the coast and the armies of the Mississippi. The North has never realized, perhaps, what it owes for its victory to this non-slaveholding southern mountaineer. (Ibid., 447–8)

Stephen G. Bowles, who served in the 14th Kentucky Cavalry, is shown here with his wife, Martha Jane Nunn Bowles. (Courtesy of the Jackson County Public Library)

PICTURED BELOW ARE MEN WHO SERVED IN THE CIVIL WAR.

Pictures of other Civil War servicemen may be found in other chapters: Alexander Frank Hays and James Hays are shown in Chapter 1; Thomas Engle and Archibald C. Lainhart are pictured in Chapter 2.

Fountain Fox, Company C 47th Kentucky Infantry. (Courtesy of Dallas Fox)

Elisha Gabbard, Private, Company E 47th Kentucky Infantry. (Courtesy of Dallas Fox)

Abraham Powell. (Courtesy of Nolan Powell)

James Robert Engle. (Courtesy of James E. Hays)

Elijah McWhorter. Company C 47th Kentucky Infantry. (Courtesy of Ronnie McWhorter)

Elbert G. Bowles, Company D of the 7th Regiment of the Kentucky Infantry Volunteers. (Courtesy of the Jackson County Public Library)

Fox's claim that all the men of Jackson County joined the Union cause is most likely exaggerated (though not by much), for there were slave holders in the county. The 1860 Slave Schedule of the U.S. Census reports seven slaves and three slave owners in the county. And, as Hutchinson reports in a Civil War Roundtable discussion, some mountaineers did own slaves, particularly in the fertile mountain valleys of North Carolina and Tennessee, where large-scale farming could benefit from slave labor. (Hutchinson, 1965)

Nevertheless, the generality stands—this was Union territory, with a strong bias against slavery. According to local historian, Jess Wilson, the anti-slavery sentiment in Jackson County was buttressed by the work of four men—Cassius Marcellus Clay, the Reverend John G. Fee, the Reverend George Candee, and Robert E. Nichols. Before the outbreak of the Civil War, the famous abolitionist, Cassius Clay, gave a speech in McKee against slavery. John Fee, a Presbyterian minister, established an abolitionist school at nearby Berea, offering education to both black and white. (This was the forerunner of Berea College.) Reverend George Candee, who settled in McKee in 1858 after being run out of Pulaski County, traveled around preaching against slavery. Robert E. Nichols, called "Radical Bob," was from Moores Creek and Pond Creek in Jackson County and the source of local legend. (Wilson, 1982)

As the story goes, there was, among the local populace of the county, a fear that a pro-slavery mob from Madison County would try an invasion of Jackson County. One day, word spread quickly (a rumor started by a drunk, they say) that the Madison County mob was on its way. Radical Bob and L. J. Robinson led twelve men into McKee ready for a confrontation, but no mob showed. Later, the Richmond paper ran a story claiming Radical Bob had sixty armed men in McKee. Of course, no one told them differently. (Ibid.)

It is not known how many men and boys from Jackson County did serve in this war, but it is likely that most families sent a man off to war. In a rural community, this left the women and children, the elderly, and the infirm to keep the farmstead going.

Local government was also affected, as newly elected officials answered the call. One such was Thomas Jefferson Engle, Jackson County's first elected county clerk. He barely completed his term of office in 1862 when he joined the 47th Kentucky Mounted Infantry. Captain Engle (whose picture may be found in Chapter 2 of this book) died in 1863 in camp and is buried in the McKee Cemetery. In addition, the reliance on citizens to keep roads in good repair must have meant neglect of roads, as able-bodied men left for war.

A letter from Levi Pennington, a lieutenant in the Union Army serving under Sherman, and ancestor to many Jackson Countians, gives a glimpse into the life and times of a Civil War soldier. He was killed in action at Chickasaw Bluffs, Vicksburg, Mississippi. Reproduced at right is his last letter home.

Camp Wolf River, near
Memphis, Tennessee
December 9, 1862

My dear wife and children and father and mother: I once more take the opportunity of writing you a few lines to let you know that I am well and have been in tolerable good health since I left you. The boys are all as well as common, except J.C. Turner who has been very sick, but he is now recovering. We have traveled a great deal since I left home. We traveled about one thousand miles on steam boats. I have been in several states since I left you. We first went from Kentucky to the Ohio River, crossed the river, and went through Ohio then 64 miles up the Kanawa River into Virginia, stayed there 12 days, then marched back to the Ohio River, then got on boats and went down the river passing the states of Ohio, Indiana, Illinois, Missouri, Arkansas and are now camped in the state of Tennessee. I have seen a great deal of good land, but I have become satisfied if I live to be discharged, and get back home, to spend the balance of my days in Jackson County Kentucky. I will proceed to give my reasons for being satisfied to live in as poor a county as Jackson. In passing through the state of Ohio I saw the happiest people I ever saw any where living on poorer land than there is in Jackson County. They had their farms all fenced in four or five acre lots, sown in grass, Clover, wheat, rye and etc. and were living good and well painted framed houses with good stables for their stock. They done their own work, and each spoke well of the others. The health of our Country is another reason why I prefer living there. The great reason is I think it is not right for people to crave riches in this world, for if a man possessed the world it would do him no good in the world to come. We had better try to lay up treasures in Heaven, where moth nor rust doth corrupt, where war, sin or sorrow, nor pain dwell, but all are one in Christ. I want you all to seek the Lord and obtain a pardon and be present to meet me in Heaven, where we will part no more. I have a good hope when I leave this earth I will meet my two children who have departed this life in Heaven. If I could only know that my wife and the rest of my children and my friends were prepared to meet me there, I would be much happier than I am. Children, above all things obey your mother, for she will give you good counsel. Rachel, try all you can to get your children to do right.

*   Levi Pennington*

P.S. I will say to that there are a great many of our troops here. It is reported that the Rebels are retreating before our men who left before we came here, and it is believed that the fighting is about done, as there are several propositions of peace. I am in command of the Company and will soon be commissioned as Captain. Col. Garrard is our General, and Col. Rigel is commanding our regiment. I have received but one letter from you since I left home. (Wilson, When They …, 1978, 61–62)

Orville Anderson Fox, Private, Company D 4th Kentucky Infantry, served in the Spanish-American War in 1898. (Courtesy of Jay Fox)

Grant Holcomb, served in the Spanish-American War of 1898. (Courtesy of Dena Lakes Burgess)

For the most part, the mountains of eastern Kentucky were spared as battlefields in this War Between the States. However, on August 23, 1862, the advance cavalry of Confederate Major General Kirby Smith's invading army engaged and defeated a small Union force at the top of Big Hill, near the congruence of Jackson, Rockcastle, and Madison Counties. This was a prelude to the larger Battle of Richmond, where Confederate forces succeeded in routing the Union Army and capturing four thousand Union soldiers. (AmericanCivil-War.com) But after the Battle of Perryville in October of 1862, the Confederate Army retreated; and Kentucky experienced no other large-scale invasions from the South. There did, however, continue to be numerous raids into the state by small marauding bands.

The aftermath of the Civil War brought changes to the political line-up in Kentucky. Jack Hutchinson, in a speech to the Cincinnati Civil War Roundtable in 1965, states:

> The Bluegrass, old stronghold of the Whig Party, became ardently Democrat together with the Pennyrile and The Purchase. The Democratic Party in the Bluegrass and western Kentucky thus became part and parcel of the solidly Democratic South and remained so until the New Deal era when there began to show definite signs of conservative reaction in the inner Bluegrass. The Mountaineers of Eastern Kentucky, on the other hand, deserted their long Jacksonian Democratic loyalty due to their unshakable allegiance to the Union and their dislike for the old slave-owning aristocracy. They adopted a sturdy Republican allegiance which remained steadfast until the New Deal Years of Franklin D. Roosevelt wooed many mountaineers back to the Democratic Party. (Hutchinson, 1965, cincinnaticwrt.org)

Jackson County is a stark example of a mountain county's long standing loyalty to the party of Lincoln. As pointed out in Chapter 9 of this book, the county has consistently supported the Republican Party, with more than eighty-five percent of the vote regularly going Republican.

THE SPANISH-AMERICAN WAR

As Spain tried to quell rebellion in Cuba, one of its possessions in 1898, an American battleship, the USS Maine, was sunk in the Havana Harbor. America declared war on Spain in April 1898, resulting in the loss of 2,300 men. In a decisive battle in the Philippines, the United

States established itself as a consequential naval power; and the Treaty of Paris in December 1898 awarded control of the Philippines, Puerto Rico, and Guam to the United States.

Although several men from Jackson County fought in this war, there are no records of deaths.

WORLD WAR I

This Great War—this War to End All Wars—this First World War resulted in forty million casualties—devastating Europe and setting the stage for World War II. There were about ten million military deaths, ten million civilian deaths, and twenty million wounded. Great Britain sustained almost one million military deaths and France over 1.3 million, compared to 382,000 and 212,000, respectively, in World War II.

The United States did not enter this European adventure until 1917, three years after its beginning and nineteen months before its close. Nevertheless, these nineteen months of war took their toll—resulting in about 120,000 deaths. It is estimated that 43,000 of these deaths were because of the Spanish influenza, a worldwide epidemic which killed more people in one year than the bubonic plague did in five years in the fourteenth century. (Billings, 1997)

The McKee draft board sent a total of 224 men, along with fourteen volunteers, to World War I. Of those 238 men, sixteen were killed in the war. (Bowles, [1919], 12). They were:

Thomas W. Azville, Clover Bottom
John C. Burgin, Bond
Clarence Chappel, Welchburg
James L. Clemmons, Sand Gap
Thurman Dunnigan, Tyner
Robert Fox, Olin
Luther Gabbard, Parrott
Charles O. Hamilton, Tyner
Alfred Harris, Parrott
John Huff, Privett
William E. Jones, Sand Gap
James F. King, Bond
Rolla Malicoat, Threelinks
Willie McQueen, McKee
John E. St. John, Egypt
John Smith, Privett

Jackson Morris, Adjutant-General for the State of Kentucky, 1920–23, and Jackson County native, served in France during World War I with the rank of major. (Courtesy of Jess Wilson)

PICTURED BELOW ARE JACKSON COUNTIANS WHO SERVED IN WORLD WAR I.

Delbert York, 1918. (Courtesy of Carolyn York)

Green Montgomery (left), 1919. (Courtesy of Tony Gabbard)

Ray Hornsby. (From the Engle Collection, courtesy of Ginny Ashonosheni)

Edward Evans in 1902 at Ft. Delaware. (Courtesy of Mary Moore)

Dillard Moore and Sherman Cunagan. (Courtesy of Mary Moore)

WORLD WAR II

The Treaty of Versailles, which ended World War I, exacted harsh economic terms from Germany, crippling the economy and leading to resentment and the rise of fascism in the 1930s. Hitler's incursions into surrounding countries were overlooked in Europe until the invasion of Poland in 1939, when war was again declared. The United States managed to occupy a position of neutrality until the Japanese attack on Pearl Harbor on December 7, 1941.

World War II drew into its orbit most countries of the world. This scope resulted in enormous losses—over 70 million, including civilian casualties and deaths from famine and disease. Although France and England saw fewer casualties than in World War I, other countries, many of whom had not been touched by the first world war, sustained unprecedented losses: over 23 million in the Soviet Union, 19 million in China, 7.5 million in Germany, 5 million in Poland, 4 million in Indonesia, 2 million in Japan. The United States lost over four hundred thousand in World War II.

In America, this war was keenly felt, with hardly a family untouched by the service of someone in the military. And civilians were involved daily. With the Second World War came the rationing of sugar, coffee, butter, meat, gasoline, tires, fuel oil, and shoes. Women were called on to work in the factories supplying the war effort, and every family was asked to assist in the war effort by collecting tin cans, growing victory gardens, and conserving resources wherever possible. A notice in *The Jackson County Sun* in 1943 asked local housewives to do their part, suggesting that they reduce the number of tin cans they used. The article pointed out that by conserving only one can a week, they would save enough steel for 1,389 machine guns. And the county government pitched in, donating the wrought iron fence around the courthouse to the war effort.

Berton J. McQueen, was killed in action during World War II. (Courtesy of Regina Brewer)

However, the greatest sacrifices came with the loss of loved ones. The story of Berton Jay McQueen (pictured at right) is the story of many. McQueen volunteered and was inducted into the U.S. Army on April 20, 1943. He was assigned to the 5th Army Company D 141 Infantry and was soon shipped overseas. His mother, Nannie McFarland McQueen, received a telegram on March 14, 1944, reporting he had been wounded. By April, he was back on active duty. Another telegram on September 12, 1944, stated that he had been wounded again in August. Again he soon returned to duty. But on December 9, 1944, Mrs. McQueen received notice that he was missing in the vicinity of Arnold, France, and on June 11, 1946, she received word that he had been killed in action, though his body was never recovered. Mrs. McQueen always had hope that her son was alive, so his allotments and life insurance money remained in the bank for

James H. Jackson is shown here in Capri on leave after his thirtieth bombing mission. Just a few months later, he and his crew were shot down in 1944. He spent the remainder of the war in a prisoner of war camp in Germany. (From the Anna Blair Collection, courtesy of JoAnne Moore)

almost fifty years after his death. Berton J. McQueen's name is on a memorial in McKee and on the Wall of the Missing in Epinol, France. (Information supplied by Regina Brewer, great niece of Berton Jay McQueen)

We offer two other stories which bring home to us, so many years later, the awful trials endured by soldiers in wartime. James H. Jackson, raised in Gray Hawk and New Zion, joined the U.S. Army Air Corps in November of 1942—just eighteen years old. After twenty months of training as an engineer on the B-17 aircraft, he was sent to Italy, completing forty-four missions before being shot down and captured in December of 1944. He and his crew were only five flights away from reaching fifty missions, which would have sent them home for extended leave. They spent the rest of the war in Stalag-Luft #1 in Barth, Germany, and were liberated by the Russians on May 7, 1945. Jackson's story of life as a prisoner of war has been preserved for us in a manuscript entitled *The James H. Jackson, Jr. Story*, written by Ernie Moore. It may be found in the Jackson County Library's Kentucky Room.

William Whicker, serving in Italy in 1944, is shown here with an Italian family who lived very near his army base. (Courtesy of Bonnie and William Whicker)

WORLD WAR II SERVICEMEN

Zenas York. (Courtesy of Carolyn York)

Bob York. (Courtesy of Carolyn York)

Bruce Hays. (Courtesy of Ruby Hays)

Wade Fox, Tec 5 U. S. Army.
(Courtesy of Dallas Fox)

Lewis Gay. (Courtesy of Jack Norris)

Shirley Fox, Pfc. Battery F.
(Courtesy of Dallas Fox)

Hershel Gabbard. (Courtesy of
Dallas Fox)

Howard Gabbard. (Courtesy of
Dallas Fox)

WORLD WAR II SERVICEMEN

Donald Turner. (Courtesy of Emmitt Turner)

Warren Fox, Corporal, 386th Field Artillery Battalion. (Courtesy of Dallas Fox)

Ross Blair. (From the Anna Blair Collection, courtesy of JoAnne Moore)

Letcher Van Winkle. (Courtesy of Wanda Renner)

William Fox. (Courtesy of Dallas Fox)

Carson Moore, with wife Mary. (Courtesy of Mary Moore)

William Whicker, local businessman, also served in World War II. His story is told by his wife, Bonnie, who recorded it in an unpublished document, entitled, *Guardian Angels in World War II*. In the excerpt below, William Whicker relates only one of the very close calls he had during service in WWII, first in North Africa and later in Italy, resulting in his very firm conviction that he did indeed have a guardian angel—there were just too many close calls:

> I left New York at 8 o'clock a.m. on Dec. 12, 1942 on the Susan B. Anthony troop ship. …We landed in Casablanca on Dec. 24th. …We, the 331st Signal Corps, landed about 2:00 a.m. in pitch black darkness and took cover anywhere we could in the fields because the Germans had been bombing this place all night long. Search lights by the U.S. troops were picking out German planes in the air and…field artillery and anti-aircraft down to fifty caliber guns were all shooting at once—shooting them down.
>
> A few nights later in the same area the Germans were laying their bombs everywhere. My buddy and I were scrambling to find a fox hole. The bombs were falling so close to us that we had to pinch ourselves to see if we were alive after each bomb fell. They were screaming over our heads and we just knew that each one would be the one that would get us. We heard one screaming as it came in and we knew that it was closer than any of the others had been. We waited the few seconds it took the bomb to land, knowing that we were going to die. When it hit—nothing happened. It was a dud!

Arby Van Winkle on the left and Oscar Van Winkle on the right, shown here with their brother, Kinus, are home on leave during World War II. (Courtesy of Wanda Renner)

Others were wounded, and some never made it home. Listed on the next page are those from Jackson County who died in World War II. This list was garnered from the War Memorial on the Jackson County Courthouse lawn and from correspondence with the Kentucky Department of Military Affairs, Military Records and Research Branch.

World War II changed the world, and those changes reached also into Jackson County. The war effort itself led people, including women, to work in the factories of the North, which were now producing war goods. And after the war, others left to seek employment off the farm. Veterans left to take

SOLDIERS FROM JACKSON COUNTY
WHO DIED IN WORLD WAR II

Marcus Abner

Donald Abrams

Vernon Adkins

Vernus Amis

Isaac V. Atkins

Edward Bowling

Woodrow Bowling

Frank Pieomallia Burgess Jr.

William Carpenter

Carl F. Castle

Russell Cole Jr.

David Collier

Donald L. Collier

Robert Cornett

Jake Cruse

Ottis Cunnagin

Marlin Daughtery

Floyd Durham

Luther Farmer

Ray Farmer

Alonzo Fields

McKinley Gabbard

Olen C. Gilbert

Lester Glenn

Rader J. Gross

William Guerra

Woodrow Harrison

Pat Hays

Oval Hillard

Earl N. Isaacs

Edwin C. Isaacs

Arvel Johnson

Elmo Jones

Ray Jones

Loyd Kerby

Ernest King

Cloyd G. Lakes

Daniel Lakes

Eugene Lamb

John Lawson Jr.

Luther Little

Stanley Lockard

Bobby McDowell

Russell McDowell

Berton J. McQueen

Homer Moore

Sherman L. Napier

Obed Noble

Lester Reynolds

Wesley Riley

Charley Robertson

Finley Robinson

Andrew Russell

Meredith Smith

Earl Tillery

Chester Ward

Claude Watts

John S. Witt

Virgil Wright

advantage of educational opportunities provided by the government. Census data show that Jackson County lost twenty percent of its population between 1940 and 1950. And another eighteen percent left in the following decade.

THE KOREAN WAR

The United States entered the conflict known as the Korean War as a part of the United Nations Command Forces when North Korea, with the aid of the Soviet Union and the People's Republic of China, invaded South Korea on June 25, 1950. Some would say that this war has never ended, and indeed, after fifty years, there has been no formal end—only a ceasefire agreement signed July 27, 1953. The United States still has troops stationed in South Korea.

The United States suffered the loss of over fifty thousand troops in the Korean War. Jackson County soldiers lost in this conflict and listed on the Jackson County War Memorial were:

George Riley

Jesse Tyra

Jack Welch

THE VIETNAM WAR

When the French were forced out of Vietnam in 1954, after a century of colonization, the country was divided into the North, supported by the Chinese communists, and a U.S. supported government in the South. In 1960, when the Communist Party established the National Liberation Front in the North, with the intention of uniting the severed country under communist rule, the United States responded with equipment and advisors sent by President Kennedy in 1961. As tensions escalated, President Johnson ordered troops to Vietnam in 1965.

The Vietnam War, the longest military conflict in U.S. history (1965 to 1975), resulted in the loss of over 58,000 Americans, with 364,000 wounded. There are no records of Jackson Countians lost in this conflict.

Bibliography

"A Cry From the Hills of Kentucky." Wilma, Kentucky: Jackson County Baptist Institute, 1928.

AmericanCivilWar.com (http://americancivilwar.com/statepic/ky/ky007.html)

Annville Institute Alumni Association. *Annville Institute, 1909–1978*. Annville, Kentucky: Annville Institute Alumni Association, 1998.

Atlas of Kentucky. P. P. Karan and Cotton Mather, editors. Lexington, Kentucky: The University Press of Kentucky, 1977.

Billings, Molly. "The Influenza Pandemic of 1918," 1997. (http://virus.stanford.edu/uda/)

Bowles, Isaac Anderson. "History of Jackson County, Kentucky," [ca.1919]. Retyped and mimeographed by the Public Relation and Power Use Department, Jackson County RECC, McKee, Kentucky, 1974

CCC Alumni Organization. "History of the Civilian Conservation Corps." (http://www.cccalumni.org/history1.html)

Carrier, Alfred. *The Flight of the Dove: Roots of Pentecost in Eastern Ky*. Privately printed, [1982]

"Circuit Riders Brought Religious Teachings to Early Kentuckians," Author unknown, 1939. *The Kentucky Explorer*, September, 2007, 46-49.

Clark, Thomas D. *A History of Kentucky*. Lexington, Kentucky: The John Bradford Press, 1960.

Clark, Thomas D. *Agrarian Kentucky*. Lexington, Kentucky: The University Press of Kentucky, 1977.

Clark, Thomas D. *Three American Frontiers; Writings of Thomas D. Clark*. Holman Hamilton, editor. Lexington, Kentucky: University of Kentucky Press, 1968.

Commonwealth of Kentucky, Department of Military Affairs, Military Records and Research Branch, Correspondence: "Jackson County Casualty Lists for World War I, World War II, and the Korean Conflict."Jackson County Public Library.

Collins, Lewis and Richard H. Collins. *History of Kentucky*. 2 volumes, 1874. Reprinted by Kentucky Imprints, Berea, Kentucky, 1976.

Collins, Robert F. *A History of the Daniel Boone National Forest, 1770–1970.* Winchester, Kentucky: U.S. Forest Service, 1975.

Cornett, Jeff. "Historic Research on Jackson Schools, Churches, Stores, Post Offices," *Kentucky Heritage; Magazine of the Kentucky Junior Historical Society,* Spring Issue, 1983, 23-26.

DeJong, F. H. "History of the Jackson County Kiwanis Club, July 1938 to September 1944." Rewritten by Jess D. Wilson, 1974. Unpublished manuscript.

Harrison, Lowell H. and James C. Klotter. *A New History of Kentucky.* Lexington, Kentucky: The University Press of Kentucky, 1997.

Hudson, Karen E. *Jackson County, Kentucky: An Architectural History of an Appalachian Community.* For Jackson County Development Association and Kentucky Heritage Council, 1996.

Hutchinson, Jack T. "Bluegrass and Mountain Laurel: The Story of Kentucky in the Civil War," The Cincinnati Civil War Round Table, November, 1965. (http://www.cincinnaticwrt.org/data/ccwrt_history/talks_text/hutchinson_kentucky.html)

Kennedy, Rachel and Cynthia Johnson. *The New Deal Builds: A Historic Context of the New Deal in East Kentucky, 1933 to 1943.* Frankfort, Kentucky: Kentucky Transportation Cabinet and Kentucky Heritage Council, n.d.

Lawson, Ruth Bingham. "Circuit Rider Robert Bingham Was a Preacher, Soldier, and Farmer," *The Kentucky Explorer,* July-August 1996, 67-68.

McCauley, Deborah Vansau. *Appalachian Mountain Religion; A History.* Urbana and Chicago: University of Illinois Press, 1995.

Moore, Ernie. *The James H. Jackson, Jr. Story.* Self-published, 2002.

Raitz, Karl and Nancy O'Malley. "Local-scale turnpike roads in nineteenth century Kentucky," *Journal of Historical Geography,* vol. 33, Issue 1, January 2007.

Rennick, Robert M. "Jackson County, Kentucky Post Offices," 1975. Unpublished manuscript.

Sasser, June. "History of Early Jackson County," 1981. Unpublished manuscript.

Sasser, June. "History of Irvine Association of Kentucky Baptists." Unpublished Manuscript.

Sasser, June. The June Sasser Collection of Church Records. The Jackson County Public Library.

Shapiro, Henry D. *Appalachia on Our Mind; The Southern Mountains and Mountaineers in the American Consciousness, 1870–1920.* Chapel Hill, North Carolina: The University of North Carolina Press, 1978.

Sharp, William E. and A. Gwynn Henderson. *Mute Stones Speak: Archaic Lifeways of the Escarpment Region in Jackson County, Kentucky.* Lexington, Kentucky: Kentucky Archaeological Survey, 1997.

Sparks, Wade Steven. "How Coal Affected Sand Gap, Kentucky; Jackson County Mining," *Kentucky Heritage; Magazine of the Kentucky Junior Historical Society,* Spring Issue, 1983, 6-7.

The Adventures of Colonel Daniel Boon, Formerly a Hunter. Xenia, Ohio: Old Chillicothe Press, 1968.

Williams, Roger. *An Unpayable Debt; History of Bond Baptist Church.* BibleLine Ministries. 1995.

Williams, Roger. *AudleyTurner: The Pilgrimage of a Lumber Camp Preacher.* Private printing, 1997.

Wilson, Jess. "It Happened Here." *The Rural Kentuckian,* February 1976, July 1976, March 1977, May 1977, April 1981, December 1982.

Wilson, Jess. *When They Hanged the Fiddler,* Berea, Kentucky: Kentucky Imprints, 1978.

Index